A WALK DOWN MISERY STREET

PETR NEMIROVSKIY

Walk Down Misery Street

Copyright ©2022 Petr Nemirovskiy

All rights reserved.

Published by Red Penguin Books

Bellerose Village, New York

Library of Congress Control Number: 2022904034

ISBN

Print 978-1-63777-346-8

No part of this book may be reproduced in any form or by any electronic or mechanical means, including information storage and retrieval systems, without written permission from the author, except for the use of brief quotations in a book review.

To Michael

PREFACE

When undertaking this book, I set a simple task before myself: to share with readers the personal experience of a man who decided to try himself in the role of a substance abuse counselor, without having any idea of what addiction really was. I wanted to let the readers know what impressions, feelings, and thoughts my experience evoked as I became closely acquainted with the closed-off and bizarre world of drug addicts in New York.

However, this facially simple task turned out to be extremely difficult. During the time of writing this book, I constantly went off on a tangent. I began to present knowledge that might be interesting and useful only to a limited number of professionals, who are working in the substance abuse field but not to a wide range of different readers. Or, conversely, I strayed into the tone of fiction, and my story gradually turned into a novel with an exciting plot, which possessed artistic merits but did not reflect the documentary angle of the reality being described.

That is why it took me about ten years to write this book! I constantly rewrote chapters and changed the protagonist's character. During this time, obviously, a lot was changing in our country, in the substance abuse field, and also in my personal life.

But the "stretching" of time for this book has been greatly

beneficial. As a result, this work reflects the gradual "growth" of the main character, both spiritually and professionally, from when he began his career as an ordinary addiction counselor to when he became a professor at a well-known university.

What is the meaning behind this title? I first heard this name from a patient; he was a gifted poet, and one of his poems about drug addiction was called "Misery Street". Indeed, over time, working in the field I began to imagine drug addiction as a symbolic street—a long and winding road. Such a street exists in any city, village, or populated area. You can find yourself on this street via various paths, each taking their own. One person might find themselves there due to a genetic predisposition to alcohol and drugs, while another came there under peer pressure, and someone else, out of curiosity. Of course, no one was going to linger on this street for long. For the first time in life, when raising a glass of wine or smoking the first blunt, no one does it to become a drug addict or an alcoholic. No one believed that it would happen to them. "It could happen to anyone else but not with me." O, ye. Some lucky ones, having been on this street for a while, sooner or later managed to get off, while others stayed there forever.

And lastly, I would like to express appreciation to the professors of Fordham University, the colleagues with whom I have worked in various clinics and hospitals of New York, as well as all of my patients. Without YOU this book would not have seen the light of day.

FOREWORD

In his new book, *A Walk Down Misery Street*, Petr Nemirovskiy serves as a compassionate witness to the diverse lives that intersect in a busy outpatient drug treatment clinic and ED at a hospital in New York City. Although the accounts are fictionalized, Mr. Nemirovskiy draws on his real-world experience as a certified substance abuse clinician to provide a unique and accessible perspective on the lives of drug users, as well as the drug treatment system in the United States—a system that many would argue is itself in dire need of rehabilitation.

The book is notable for taking a holistic perspective on the phenomenon of drug addiction, addressing a broad range of issues, from the underlying worldview Mr. Nemirovskiy sees as common to users of a myriad of psychoactive substances to philosophical questions regarding why people use drugs, to the history of substance abuse treatment in the United States and its connections with the criminal justice system, and more.

With an eye for vivid detail and compelling characters, Mr. Nemirovskiy communicates these underlying themes through a series of engaging anecdotes, making both the patients and fellow staff members he encountered in his work come alive for the reader. The themes he addresses in *A Walk Down Misery Street* are particularly relevant today, as the United States is experiencing disconcerting increases in heroin use, driven in large part by the over-prescription of opioid-based pharmaceutical painkillers, and observers on various points of the political spectrum are questioning the wisdom of the War on Drugs.

The author's decision to frame the narrative with a personal account of his experience, how he came to work with people with substance use problems, adds important context and depth to the stories and character sketches. His personal narrative not only humanizes the author, but is also especially engaging and relatable, and is likely to appeal to a broad range of readers, drawing them into the book.

As a public health researcher who focuses on drug use, I enthusiastically recommend this book to anyone who has been touched by addiction or anyone who is interested in reading a sensitive and original take on the issue.

Honoria Guarino, Ph.D.,
Principal Investigator,
Public Health Researcher

CONTENTS

PART ONE

- 3   IN THE CAPITAL OF THE WORLD
- 7   HOPELESS PHILOSOPHER
- 9   WORKING AS A SECURITY GUARD: THE ART OF DOING HOURS
- 13   DRUG COUNSELING SCHOOL
- 15   SYLVIA, THE LIONESS
- 21   THE PETER BROTHERS
- 29   KEVIN: THE RIDDLE OF THE SPHINX
- 37   STRANGE VISIONS
- 39   "LOOK AT THE TRASHCAN!"
- 41   THE SCARECROW IN FRONT OF THE UNIVERSITY
- 45   SCHOOL IS OUT—INTO THE WORLD!
- 51   MY DEAR AUNT

PART TWO

- 55   THE FIRST JOB: "WHAT AM I DOING HERE?"
- 59   LIZA: THE SWEET LADY THAT COULD
- 73   DON'T BELIEVE YOUR LYING EYES!
- 79   VETERAN ADAM: WAR THAT NEVER ENDS
- 85   "NOT EVEN A DOLLAR"

PART THREE

- 93   A FEMININE FACE
- 95   CHARMING CYNTHIA
- 103   WALKING ON THE EDGE
- 109   "PEE-PEE TIME": DRAMA IN THE RESTROOM
- 113   UNDERGROUND CITY
- 115   CRAPPY PORTFOLIO
- 123   WORKING IN ED

125 "YELLOW GOWNS"
129 DR. DJ
131 PHYSICIAN, HEAL THYSELF
133 WAR ZONE
135 THE CHILDREN OF THE GHETTO
139 "I WANT YOU TO SPELL SOMETHING FOR ME, JIM"

PART FOUR

143 KEEP GOING, STUDENT!
151 OF SEX, ROMANCE, AND AIDS
153 RED STRIPE
157 WORKING WITH THE LGBTQ COMMUNITY
161 POETRY OF DON JUAN
165 CRIME AND PUNISHMENT
167 WAR ON DRUGS
173 THE CRIMINAL WORLD
177 "WATCH YOUR BACK, COUNSELOR"
181 OVERDOSE—ONE HUNDRED PER DAY

185 EPILOGUE
189 FOOTNOTES AND AUTHOR COMMENTARY
195 ABOUT THE AUTHOR

To protect and maintain the privacy of all patients and clinicians, names, places, and locations have been changed.

PART ONE

IN THE CAPITAL OF THE WORLD

I came to America with the green card I'd won in a lottery. No bribes or fake marriages here. Such things do happen. When I won the green card, I took it as a kind of sign from God and left with little hesitation.

My life in Russia never seemed to move forward. Firstly, I did not like the political regime there. In addition, I couldn't understand who I was or what my calling was. What I knew about myself was that I liked to read novels and ponder over life; that is why I enrolled at the College of Science and Art, with a major in philosophy. But after studying there for three years, I became disillusioned with classical philosophy and dropped out of college without getting a diploma. Then, I worked as an agent at an advertising agency, and then as a proofreader in a publishing house. None of these jobs brought me much money or any fulfillment. And despite all of this, in my heart of hearts, I always believed that my life should be unique, that God had a special plan for me, and that I certainly had a mission on this Earth.

Imagine the enthusiasm and joy with which I packed my belongings to go to the States! I didn't doubt that I could quickly find my place in America, the country of unlimited opportunities. There, in the United States, all of my potentials would actualize and I would flourish.

What can I say? This is how we—humans—are built! We hope that a change of scenery will fundamentally change us, and most certainly for the better—"The Geographical Cure."

Finding myself in New York, I quickly realized that the situation here is very different from what I expected. All my hopes and illusions were quickly dashed. I had nowhere to go. I was in a foreign country, basically penniless, with poor English and no college degree. I couldn't even get a job as a grocery stock boy.

Once, having rescued a half-broken rocking chair from the sidewalk, I sat in my tiny half-basement apartment on the edge of the Capital of the World—in Brooklyn, Brighton Beach. I rocked back and forth, accompanied by the squeaking wood, and deliberated my next step.

Was it really my fate to perpetually seek something and wind up with nothing? Would I ever find my calling? I had no idea what to do. I felt like a helpless puppy, abandoned on a dark street in an unfamiliar city.

I didn't know a soul in America at that time. There was only one person in New York to whom I could turn: a distant relative of my mother (her second cousin's wife). I called her and asked if we could meet and talk. For some reason, she chose to meet at a pub.

Nestled at the bar, I asked for her advice: What profession should I choose? "Tell me, my dear aunt, what do you think?" I asked with a humorous tone.

Treating me to a fine cocktail, she without hesitation advised, "My dear Peter, why don't you become a drug counselor? Treat drug addicts and alcoholics!" Ironically, she raised her glass in a toast, as if the matter was settled and all that remained was to drink to it. "I myself have been a drug counselor for many years. It's really not difficult."

I was a little confused by what I was seeing and hearing. This sweet lady, a drug counselor, is sipping on her second cocktail and advising me to treat alcoholics? There was something very off about this picture.

I uttered, "But I don't really have any specialized education. I've never used drugs. I only drink occasionally."

"Listen, in America, you only need to study for about a year to get your substance abuse certificate. You don't need any specialized medical training. The salary isn't that high, but it's good enough to keep a roof over your head. Besides, in your own words, you like to ponder about life. You can't imagine how addicts like to philosophize, better than professors at any university. I believe that the substance abuse clinic is your rightful place. I'm sure you'll be great at it."

As I parted ways with my relative, I thought to myself: Can I really become a substance abuse counselor? Hmm... I suddenly remembered the names of some of my favorite writers—Hemingway and Fitzgerald—and many famous rock idols for whom drugs were a big part of life and led them to a tragic ending. To become a substance abuse counselor, I'm going to deal with interesting, creative people who can still be saved.

I was also thinking that for a period of time my dad heavily abused alcohol, and because of this, our family life was so harsh. I knew from my own experience how much suffering alcohol brings into people's lives.

And this work seemed aligned with my faith, specifically the Christian sentiments of fairness and compassion.

Okay, let's give it a try. Go ahead.

HOPELESS PHILOSOPHER

It was one of those Queens neighborhoods where I imagine any well-dressed man would be uncomfortable during the day and downright terrified at night. Even the trains roaring across the tracks seemed to me in a hurry to pass through. I kept noticing suspicious characters hanging around street corners and bodegas, their eyes hidden behind sweatshirt hoodies or baseball caps.

And at one intersection: the sparkling, brand-new three-story Institute for Substance Abuse Counseling. This was my new alma mater!

After completing the interview and reviewing my application, the Assistant Director, Teri, who at first glance seemed a somewhat distant and arrogant woman, handed me a booklet with a list of classes and the rules of conduct for the Institute. She firmly warned me that there is no drug use on the premises of the school and violators would be dismissed immediately. It sounded very strange to me because I was going there to study and not use drugs. She quoted the tuition fee and I agreed with the terms. Then she congratulated me on my acceptance. When we were parting, curiosity got the best of her and she asked:

"Tell me, Peter: Why are you doing this? You seem like an intelligent man."

"What do you mean?" I asked her.

"Well, it's all . . . drug addicts, alcoholics . . ." she grimaced.

"Aren't they troubled souls in need of help?" I responded, not understanding why the assistant director would say such a thing and with such a look of squeamishness.

"I see, I see." She looked at me both pensively and sympathetically.

I felt that she saw me as a hopeless romantic and philosopher who had no idea what he was getting himself into.

WORKING AS A SECURITY GUARD:
THE ART OF DOING HOURS

I was accepted to the school. It was a good step, but how to make ends meet and how to pay for this education?

Already having a prior unsuccessful attempt to get a job as a grocery stock boy, I started thinking about where I would be hired. What if I tried to be a security guard?

This time I hit the bull's eye. It turned out that it was very easy to land the job of a security guard. All you needed was a high school diploma or a GED, plus a few lectures for a hundred dollars. Also, you needed to have a clean record, not dirtied by criminal affairs. I had all this. In a few days, having listened to the lectures and paying a hundred bucks, I received the certificate of a security guard and was ready to stand guard in the capital of the world, adding to the army of thousands of security guards, with whom New York is teeming like cockroaches.

I quickly put together a resume, where I wrote that until recently I had worked as a traffic police officer in Russia.

The next day in the tabloid's "help wanted" section I chose the first "security guard wanted" listing with "no experience or references required." I called there and was invited for an interview right away at a large company which supplies contract guards in various city locations.

The interviewer, glancing briefly at my resume, inquired why

I needed this job. I lied that I was a traffic police officer in Russia and it was my cherished dream to become a cop in New York. However, as I said, I was not yet ready to be a cop in New York, because I had lived here for a short while and this job had many requirements which would take me a long time to meet. But I have to pay my bills now, and this is why I am here, looking for a job as a security guard.

Apparently, the boss liked my guileless, honest explanation. After all, I could not convince him that I dreamed of working as a security guard all my life!

"Okay, man, you're hired, for 15.50 bucks an hour. It is a decent salary for a first job. I am sending you to a great spot."

Right after the interview in the office, I was handed a uniform, gray wide pants, a heavy jacket, a visor with an emblem, a winter jacket, and two white shirts. The next evening, I was on my way to my new job, which the boss referred to as the "great spot."

This great spot turned out to be a five-story supermarket in the famous Time Warner skyscraper on Columbus Circle. My new supervisor greeted me there and, after a brief introduction, commanded me to go to the Security Operations Center to get a walkie-talkie and then quickly get back to patrolling the first floor. Thirty minutes later, I was walking along the wide corridors, from the revolving doors at one end of the corridor to the door on the other end, eyeing the shop window displays.

The shops were closing, and patrons were exiting the supermarket. I was walking around, waiting for the action to start. I expected that I would be restraining law-breakers every hour, chasing thieves, and discovering terrorists. However, it was quiet and calm there. I kept roaming, waiting for when I would start doing something specific. Yet on the first day, I had no clue what my new job entailed, its essence. I didn't expect that when one became a security guard, he would find himself in a purely surreal world of what security guards call "making hours." "How many hours did you do today?" "How many hours do you plan to make tomorrow?", etc. These commonplace phrases are found in the security guards' vocabulary.

While patrolling the empty corridor I started singing my favorite songs. "Yesterda-a-ay, all my troubles seemed so far awa-a-ay..." "Mama-a, I just killed a ma-an..."

I recalled the times when I was crazy about Western rock music as a teenager in Russia. I often visited the record store where they sold some electronics, vinyl records, and CDs with patriotic Russian songs. Usually, there were not a lot of visitors, but outside the store were always scalpers and music fanatics, modestly holding cheap burlap sacks in their hands, with recordings from the Beatles, the Doors, and Queen concerts. The rare records, discs, and posters were sold or exchanged.

Close by in the alley, there were undercover policemen closely watching the sellers of western propaganda. Sometimes they staged raids, taking everyone to the police station (the sellers and the buyers). I was also arrested a few times and taken to the police station, and then my parents and school's principal were informed that I am a reckless student and not a Russian patriot, but a traitor to my homeland.

My nostalgic memories were interrupted by screams into the walkie-talkie:

"First floor! Wake up! What is the situation there?" It was the shift supervisor returning me to reality, and in the blink of an eye, I was mentally transported from the record store in Russia to the first-floor supermarket in the Time Warner skyscraper in New York.

"Everything is ok here. Calm and quiet."

Upon finishing my evening shift, I got into the subway and got home around 1:30 at night. The next morning, having slept for five hours, I traveled to Queens, to the Institute for Substance Abuse Counseling for my first class.

DRUG COUNSELING SCHOOL

When I first crossed the threshold of the auditorium and quietly took a seat, I felt baffled. There was a lecture going on. I was expecting to see a room full of thoughtful, enlightened individuals brought here, like me, by a noble desire to do good and save the lost.

Instead, I was met with a lot of noisy commotion. I was overwhelmed by the sight and sounds, and I didn't get a good look at my classmates. I was secretly hoping I had entered the wrong auditorium. I decided at the first break to go and find my noble and refined classmates.

A somewhat nondescript teacher was giving the lecture. Students were constantly joking, and the auditorium frequently erupted into laughter. My English was poor at the time. I knew little slang, so I didn't get most of the jokes. The only words I could make out through the flood of chaotic speech were "fuck" and "shit"—the two swear words resounded throughout the auditorium. Even when everyone was silent, including the professor, the words "fuck" and "shit" kept ringing in my ears. Most of the male students wore beards and mustaches and were covered in tattoos. Their smiles seemed predatory. Many of the women looked disheveled and roughed up. What was wrong with them? Are these my classmates? Why did they look like they just had been released from jail?

My hunch about them wasn't too far from the truth, as I learned later. The hope that I'd mistakenly entered the wrong auditorium was dashed. I had come to the right place, where yesterday's drug addicts are metamorphosed into tomorrow's substance abuse counselors.

I soon learned that the government was paying for their education. According to US labor laws, people with chemical dependence are categorized as disabled and therefore have the right to free education at training programs and even colleges. The main requirement to study in a substance abuse school on a government grant is that a drug user has to be clean—free of any junk or alcohol for at least three months.

"Is it fair and just? While one person has to work as a security guard and stand still for hours in the supermarket, counting every penny to pay for his education, another, who has been getting high for years, learns for free?!" This was my initial angry reaction.

SYLVIA, THE LIONESS

Of the whole group of twenty people, only three, including me, were not in recovery.[1] Now I'll introduce you to several students in recovery.

I'll start with Sylvia, as I found myself sharing a desk with her on the very first day of school.

She was an American of Italian descent, about fifty, with luxurious black hair and in good shape for her age. I was soon surprised to learn that she wasn't fifty, but . . .forty! Sylvia retained some charm, but her beauty was obviously fading. It struck me that, had she not picked up the syringe twenty years earlier, Sylvia would have escaped misfortune and still be driving herds of lustful men crazy. But in life, unfortunately, "coulda, shoulda, woulda" don't exist, and we can only speak of what we have now, not of what could have been.

Still, Sylvia tried to maintain her image as a lioness, portraying herself as a sort of socialite. She dressed provocatively: short skirts and tight blouses.

On the second day of classes, during break, this lioness went on the hunt, and I was her intended prey. When we were left alone in the auditorium, Sylvia began to inquire about who I was and where I was from. She talked about herself, intriguingly raising her eyelids and leaning toward me so closely that our foreheads almost touched. I didn't even notice how she had caught hold of my hand—whether to shake it or to press it to her chest. By the second break, I already knew that Sylvia was single and lived in a studio apartment in Brooklyn. Her thirteen-year-old daughter was living with her mother in New Jersey and she had divorced her husband a while ago. And . . . she was completely free this evening after school!

I wasn't prepared for such rapid development in a relationship. All I knew was I had to rush to the other side of the city to patrol the supermarket in the Time Warner building.

Sylvia found my excuses unconvincing, especially when she learned I was a bachelor. She continued her hunt for the next several days. She would move close to me for any reason. She played with the button on her shirt and invited me to her place "for coffee."

I remember Sylvia's wide-open eyes when we did our first assignment together, and I brought up famous writers and philosophers, even mentioning something about the United Nations. The longer I spoke, recalling such "weird" names and references that were as distant to her as faraway planets, the wider Sylvia's eyes got. Then it hit her! She finally understood who was sitting next to her. A bookworm!

Upon her realization, Sylvia decided to correct her error without delay. She had wasted a whole week on someone she thought was only playing around, pretending to be a "goody-two-shoes." But he really was one!

The next day Sylvia fluttered away, like a butterfly, to another desk, to another male student. Actually, I had thought of her as a lioness, not a butterfly, and this comparison seemed more accurate. Soon she had this other guy wrapped around her finger.

All the students and teachers observed the growth of their sweet romance for several months—how they helped each other cheat on the exams, how they walked to the café together during breaks, and how after classes she would get in his car and theatrically slam the door shut. They'd talk about how crazy happy they were since they met each other, and thanked God for bringing them together in this auditorium!

Soon enough, they began to skip classes together. After one particularly long absence, Sylvia finally reappeared. Her face was very pale and her eyes were cloudy and glazed. Sylvia barely found the strength to sit. She'd prop up her chin with her hands all the time, drooping forward, almost resting on the desk, sweating, shivering as if she was freezing. Cliché as it sounds, she looked . . . like a cold turkey. Her black, uncombed hair contrasted with her porcelain-white face. She had on a worn jacket. She stared blankly at the board, where the teacher was writing something.

Only now I can imagine how she was struggling. Poor Sylvia, whose joints were aching, leg muscles wrenching, stomach-churning. She had to hide her cloudy, doped-up eyes from the students and teachers. But they all knew: Sylvia had relapsed! In addition, she dragged her boyfriend into the abyss with her and he also picked up drugs. Why did he need her? He would have been better off studying alone.

Everyone was looking at Sylvia. Was she still a goddess, a lioness-socialite? Or was she now your so-called useless, dirty junkie? How embarrassing it must be!

Sylvia didn't finish school. She relapsed several times, then finally gave up coming to classes altogether. The thousands of dollars that the government granted her as a scholarship were wasted.

Then I started to realize that my angry reaction against the distribution of government funds to help drug addicts in getting professional education was very superficial. The real problem is not that the government funds are distributed unfairly (as some allege), but that even with such generous support a good percentage of drug users were not able to change their life and after unsuccessful attempts returned to the dreadful world from which they came.

Before I finish with Sylvia, I have to mention one more incident that perplexed me greatly.

During a class, Sylvia raised her hand to answer a question posed by the teacher. Then she unexpectedly spoke openly in front of the whole group on a topic apparently unrelated to the lesson.

"My older cousin molested me when I was thirteen. I haven't been able to have a normal relationship with a man since. I live with shame. I've been sexually promiscuous from the time I was seventeen. I've never considered myself a normal woman. I was embarrassed and hated myself. I hated men and I feared them. I dreamed of meeting my ideal man and becoming his true friend, but I lived like a prostitute! Then heroin entered my life..."

I was in shock. I hadn't imagined it was possible—a young, thirty-nine-year-old woman speaking before a group of strangers about what would be hard to say even to one's closest friends and family! She cried, practically howled.

The students' reactions also impressed me. Some paid close attention to her, knowingly nodding their heads. Others half-listened, and still others utilized the pause in the lecture to sneak a peek at their iPhone.

Listening to Sylvia's confession, I simultaneously felt compassion and a kind of distaste for her. I had no doubt her story was true, yet something unnecessary, even artificial, came in through her revelation. What made her share it in front of everybody, with her boyfriend present?

In the not-too-distant future, I, like any substance abuse counselor, would often hear similar outpourings from women (and from men, too, by the way) who were molested. At the time, however, I was taken aback and bewildered.

Remembering Sylvia today, I can see the connections between her relapses and her public sharing. It was not coincidental. She was comprised of two halves: Sylvia the drug user who "lived like a prostitute," and Sylvia the young girl who was molested. These were the only two ways she knew herself. Every time she tried to kick the drugs, she encountered this "stained and denigrated" girl who hated herself with all her soul.

What was the meaning of her confession? Was it just for

show, an attempt to draw attention? Or was it a cry of despair before a coming relapse?

She left the Institute and I never saw her again.

There are many Sylvias, with very similar stories and nearly the same destinies, who cross the threshold of substance abuse clinics every day in America and other countries.

I'll say more about female drug users in due course.

THE PETER BROTHERS

As soon as Sylvia left me, a man by the name of Peter sat next to me. My namesake. He looked to be about forty-seven, but it would soon be revealed that he was thirty-eight.

Seeing as this is the second time I've mentioned a discrepancy between age and appearance, I'll tell you that the majority of drug users look older than their years. Some in the drug world believe that heroin users look younger than their age, allegedly because heroin has a "freezing" effect on the aging process. This is a myth. A fifty-year-old male heroin user, if he lives to such an age, looks like a very old man. It was difficult for me to believe that the majority of the students were my peers, ages thirty-five to forty, but looked at least a decade older. In their complexion and facial expressions, one saw old age, weathering, and sickness. Sickness was particularly true because many students suffered from serious chronic illnesses: hypertension, diabetes, asthma. A few of them had AIDS. Moreover, because most of them had been clean for only several months, the alcohol and drugs have not yet fully evaporated from their pores—not to mention their brains.

So, then there was Peter. He had a good build, straightforward and angular facial features, and short light brown hair neatly combed to one side. The reddish bristle around his mouth and on his chin gave Peter a somewhat aristocratic look. He smiled broadly, showing his uneven yellowed teeth. Or to put it more accurately, he didn't smile—he snarled.

At that time, he told me he and his wife were in the process of divorcing. He worked the night shift as an assistant to a substance abuse counselor at a rehab clinic. He took me under his wing. As a "psychologist" (his degree earned at the University of Real Life), he immediately had me pegged as a guy who knew nothing about the drug world but was academically strong.

Soon Peter admitted to me that, once upon a time, he had smoked a lot of weed and now had memory problems as a consequence. I didn't know if it was from the grass or not, but Peter really couldn't remember many of the technical names and clinical terms that we students needed to know.

Peter and I had a mutual regard since the day we met. He started calling me his "Russian brother," and I assumed the role of his "helper." I helped him with the quizzes and exams as well as I could.

By contrast, Peter (salute to him!) was like a walking encyclopedia. He knew words and terms that were not found on examinations, but often slipped off the lips of both students and teachers: dope, boy, coke, blue, sour, booze, blow, and so on. In short, the unabridged dictionary of an American addict opened up to me, and there were so many priceless treasures!

"What's dope?" I asked Peter, hearing a brand-new word.

He smiled broadly, spreading his thick reddish scruff to each side. He looked at me with the kind of love a father must feel when he watches the first steps of his one-year-old son.

"Dope—this is heroin, my friend. You know, the grayish powder in a little plastic bag."

"Aha. And what's coke?"

"That's cocaine. It's also a powder, but it's white. You must remember, my Russian brother, dope is usually injected and coke is usually snorted." Peter enigmatically held a thick index finger under his nose and pressed his large nostril on one side. His whole face grimaced. "Will you remember? Don't get them confused."

In his voice, I heard the emphatic irony of a parent: he had to tell me about things—the pipes for smoking crack, the syringes, the pills—things that even today's schoolchildren know. Just like a good teacher, Peter was patient. Several times he showed me how to snort imaginary coke, roll a joint, or cook and shoot dope.

That's how we helped each other at school.

Peter loved to joke around and laughed a lot. He was down-to-earth and happy-go-lucky. As they say, he was an open book. But sometimes I noticed a deep sadness flicker in his eyes, an incomprehensible longing, and a melancholy so poignant it was painful to look at him, for he concealed something deep in his heart.

Our classmates called us the Peter Brothers. We had lunch together in the diner. Sometimes I complained to him that I understood little, if nothing, of this subject of drug addiction, and that it was probably in vain that I came to this field of study. Maybe it wasn't my cup of tea. Homesickness began to gnaw at me. More and more, I recalled my home in Russia, my parents, our garden, and the river where as a kid I had gone swimming and fishing with my friends. I was feeling like a stranger among these coarse, noisy students who were always chuckling at something I never could comprehend. They looked at me as if I was a weird overseas creature carried by some random wind to their land.

Once during a conversation, I noticed something off with Peter. He was walking next to me, responding "yes-yes" to my comments, but he clearly wasn't hearing me. We walked to the diner and Peter was behind me the whole time for some reason. I turned around. Was this the same Peter? The jolly fellow, the jokester? No, I saw a haggard, pale, old man. He could barely keep up with me. He was trembling all over, his shoulders shaking and his head quivering on his tense neck.

"Peter, what's wrong?" I asked, alarmed.

"I'm fine, bro. I didn't get any sleep last night. I had a lot of work," he answered, looking off to the side.

Having seen Sylvia with her dope-sick cloudy eyes not too long ago, I now looked at shivering pale Peter, and I saw a striking similarity. In that moment, I recalled what we were learning in school. I sensed what was causing his condition. Drug withdrawal! This is what drug withdrawal looks like.

Peter was able to graduate from the Institute and receive his diploma. For all his openness, he never let me into his personal life. He would offer half-hints about difficult and painful divorce proceedings and often talked about his problems in general.

After the Institute we kept in touch, but less and less over time. It turned out we had little to talk about. Our studies had ended, our mutual assistance was no longer required, and sympathy wasn't sufficient to evolve our relationship into a friendship. Soon Peter stopped taking my calls.

We met again a few years after graduation. I was working in an outpatient substance abuse clinic, and here comes Peter—as a patient. I saw from the documentation he gave me that he had been in prison for six months for beating his ex-wife. The beating happened two years before, but, for various reasons, the verdict was postponed and only this year the judicial red tape was resolved. Peter was sentenced to a half-year in prison, served his time, and was released that day.

The next paper he handed me revealed the cause of the deep sadness I had often seen in his eyes. Pete was living with AIDS.

He told me the rest of his story. He was referred to the drug clinic on his way out of prison. He had no place to live and no money.

He looked the same as before: thick red hair and bristles around his mouth. His beard was thicker, but he no longer had the look of aristocracy. He did smile in the way he always had, with open yet slightly mischievous eyes.

Peter sensed right away that I was no longer a rookie who needed to be told that you shoot dope and you snort coke. He could see that his "Russian brother" was already immersed in this world of misery and desperation.

"Pete, my Russian brother! How have ya been?!" he exclaimed, not showing any sign of surprise at our unexpected meeting.

I saw no hint of envy or shame in Peter's expression. Who was he now, a "homeless, ex-convict, AIDS-infected junkie"?

By this time, I knew that drug users don't display their shame in the same way as "regular" people. It's hard for many of us to imagine the kind of senseless and desperate acts drug users sometimes commit because they are ashamed.

Peter and I embraced, slapping one another on the shoulders.

"Bro, look how we ran into each other just like that!"

We briefly recalled our days of student life and studies.

"I haven't lost everything in my life yet! I've still got something left," Peter said as I filled out his intake forms. "I have the two most important things in life," he announced, holding up his fist. "For one, I'm alive." He emphatically put up his index finger. "And for another, I have God." Another finger went up. Then he made a fist again and pumped it over his head as if he'd just won a significant battle. "Life and God! You see?"

I nodded approvingly, impressed with his resilience. What a guy, I thought. He seemingly lost everything but is keeping the faith. Life hasn't hardened him, and he hasn't given up his soul. I neither judged nor blamed him. But I also did not pity him.

Smiling broadly (his smile was even more wolfish since prison), Peter suddenly thrust his hand into his backpack and took out a folder with different documents from prison and photographs. He found the picture he wanted: he and I together at the Institute at the graduation ceremony. We were standing together, arms around each other, diplomas in hand.

"Wow! The Peter Brothers. I don't have one like it. Let me take a shot." I said.

"Sure, take it."

I took my cell and shot a picture.

I didn't ask Peter about his AIDS or his ex-wife or prison.

That would have been too much for our first encounter. And what was the hurry? There was so much time ahead of us, I thought. A few other patients awaited me in the hall. The director stuck his head into my office with an expression as if to say, "why are you taking so long?"

I handed to Peter a list of local food pantries that gave free food to the poor and homeless. I called a sober house and arranged a place for him to stay.

"This is just the first step. We'll file a housing application, based on your medical things with AIDS. With time you can get a job in a substance abuse clinic somewhere. You've still got your diploma and work experience."

He nodded, making a fist as a sign of his full determination to fight and win. He kept his somewhat strained eyes on me, as if in expectation. I looked at the closed door. I put my hand in my pocket and took out two crumpled twenties.

"Take it. You can give it back whenever."

Peter took the money, sighing lightly as if relieved. Then he pensively furrowed his brow.

Of course, he knew that substance abuse counselors, like all workers in any drug clinic, including secretaries and janitors, were strictly forbidden to give patients any money. Peter would have understood had I not given him a cent. He had nothing to lose, but I could get into trouble at work. Regardless of how nice and honest a patient may appear, crossing a professional boundary into a purely human interaction carries a risk, especially concerning money.

Still, I believe Pete expected this from me—this well-meaning though arguably unprofessional act. He didn't have a dime. Only a subway card. And his life. And God.

He hid the money in his pocket. He was in worn-out sneakers, ripped jeans, and an old sweater. We hugged again and agreed to meet the next morning.

Peter didn't show up the next morning, or the following week. He never showed up at the halfway house I had arranged for him. His cell was disconnected. I had no way of finding out what happened to him or where he went. All that was left in my cell was the picture of us together—students at graduation.

What happened to him? Why did he disappear? Had I done the right thing in giving a chronic drug user, just released from prison, forty dollars? Such a sum amounted to four bags of heroin or cocaine.

"You snort coke, shoot dope. Make sure you don't get them confused, my Russian brother."

Did he buy himself a hot dog and some sneakers, or those damned bags of drugs? Had he gotten high and landed himself back in prison? Was giving him money an act of good or evil? When dealing with drug addiction, common sense and ethical principles are often challenged, if not turned upside down.

I never learned any details of his terrible illness and his domestic violence criminal case. Did his ex-wife by any chance infect him?

What's with him now? Where is he?

God help him!

KEVIN: THE RIDDLE OF THE SPHINX

Kevin was a mystery. Nobody could figure him out. He was a riddle to our group. After Sylvia's revelation about her molestation, the endless stream of public confessions continued until graduation. By the end, all of the students knew who was molested, who had what illness, and who had done time in prison.

Over time, I came to appreciate the different aspects of this sharing.

Drug users and alcoholics who have been in treatment engage in psychotherapy, either individual or group, where open confession is a key factor in their recovery. Clinicians encourage their patients: "Don't keep it inside! Don't hold any secrets within! Let go of what you are hiding! You are as sick as your secrets."

In my first years working with drug users, I couldn't help but sense that I was entering a world not of real people, but of some type of ghosts. I observed that drug users love mystery. They love the shadows and the twilight. They hate the light. They won't remove their sunglasses, even on winter evenings. Baseball caps are pulled low over their eyes. They cover their heads with hoods in sunny weather. They wear dark clothing. They prefer cars with tinted windows. Light is their arch-enemy. Drug users are night people, nocturnal like moths. They don't fly in the light but distance themselves from it as if it is their worst foe. They need to hide things and hide themselves, even when it seems unnecessary. They complicate and befuddle everything they can, and they create mysteries out of nothing and then carry these mysteries in the gloom of their wailing souls, where they can nurture the monsters.

Unfortunately, sharing with others is no guarantee of success. The fact is that such revelations become routine. It may be difficult to disclose something shameful for the first time and maybe even the second. By the third time, disclosure is a little easier. By the fourth time, you are already used to it. Such disclosure in and of itself no longer becomes helpful, because you may not be concerned about connecting with painful feelings anymore, but rather with just impressing your audience. How striking it is to stand before everyone and proclaim: "Because of dope, I cheated on my husband with a famous baseball player" or "I sold crack and was shot three times, but by some miracle, I survived." Wow!

Moreover, just as a maestro works on his composition, many drug users often change parts of their confessional stories slightly to sound a little more artful, like writing for a dramatic film or novel. (Writers and screenwriters who lack inspiration and plots could find in any addiction clinic an inexhaustible source of creativity for any genre—from soap operas to action films).

Unlike the other students, Kevin was a man of few words. He responded to questions briefly and without theatrics.

He was an American of Norwegian descent. Clean-shaven, he was always neat in appearance, punctual and polite. He rarely kept the conversation alive. He was a quick study, passing every exam on the first try.

But Kevin's stubborn unwillingness to answer the question of whether or not he used drugs evoked general irritation and even some anger from the students. They posed this question to Kevin from the first day to the last day of school. Everyone asked him about it—first the students, then even several teachers. Yet Kevin remained enigmatically silent on the matter. If he was answering a question on the board, for example, on pharmacology or some other topic, someone would always take the opportunity to ask him: "C'mon and tell us: Are you in recovery? Did you use?"

Kevin would shrug, with a look of regret on his face.

"I can't answer. Sorry, this is personal," he would say with a sigh, and everyone in the auditorium would shoot him a dirty look, thinking:

What a timid one! So sly! He was clearly one of us—a junkie. Why should he contort himself into the semblance of a normal man? Why pretend? Does he think he's better than us? No way! He is cut from the same cloth. He's from the very same dirty, corrupt, screwed-up world we are! Or . . . is he?

Kevin worked as a counselor in a rehab clinic. He was a teacher by profession, but about a year ago quit the school job and entered the substance abuse field. In the clinic where he was now working, his boss required him to get a diploma as a substance abuse counselor.

I don't know how others saw him, but to me, Kevin was an ordinary young man, educated and with good manners. If I hadn't met him at this school, it wouldn't even occur to me to fish out whether he was an addict. Also incomprehensible to me were the fervor and insolence with which my classmates attempted to extract this information from him, demanding an answer to a question that, in my view, carried little if any weight: "Are you in recovery?"

What a shallow view! How could I not understand that two distinct worlds existed: the world of the addicts and—as drug users themselves refer to it—the world of the "normies"? Who separated these two worlds? Who had drawn a thick line—no, dug out a trench—between them? The users themselves, who had once upon a time crossed over this border? Or the "normies," who cast off these sick, dangerous folks who do not wish to follow the rules of society?

Who created this world of addicts? What are its law and culture? Day after day I started to see the fuller picture.

Drug users form a kind of fraternity, a commune, an order, where everyone is accepted at any age, gender, and status—teenagers and seniors, men and women, the highly educated and the illiterate, the working and the unemployed, the single and the married. Good, gentle, sentimental people. And you will meet true monsters as well.

Within this brotherhood, within this order, there is no mutual affection. They may steal from each other, despise, betray, and kill one another. But the bottom line is that anyone who has crossed the line into drug addiction enters this brotherhood, whether he wishes to or not.

Yes, an addict can detect the special scent of a fellow addict. It's enough for him to notice a fleeting glance, a word, a vocal intonation, a barely discernible movement of the lips or brows of his companion to identify that before him stands a brother. He too is an addict, someone who understands, like nobody else on Earth.[1]

Once addicted to alcohol or a drug, a half-pint of vodka or a bag of heroin—put on a scale by your sick soul—will outweigh everything else in your life: the well-being of family, professional career, personal health, and even life itself. This is what definitely separates the addict from the "normal world."

The world is hostile to the drug users, has no love for them, fears them, and doesn't believe them. We kick addicts and alcoholics out of their homes and fire them from their jobs. We take away their children. The police follow them and put them in jail. Judges bang their gavels after issuing harsh sentences.

The whole world is against them.

Thus, the question put to Kevin—Are you an addict or not?—is not an idle one, but rather of primary importance, to be understood as follows: "Are you with us or with them? If you're with them, Mister Kevin, so be it and best regards! If you are with us, then you are our brother—welcome to the family with much love!"

At that time, though, I still could not imagine what effort, professional skill, and human compassion would be required for me to gain access into this closed order, into this rough brotherhood, where they accept their own—even the lowest of scoundrels—without discussion or condition, while outsiders from the "normal" world, even sweet as angels, are accepted with great caution.

Addicts live in a lawless world like lonely wolves, each for his own survival of the fittest. At the same time, you cannot imagine the depth of empathy and compassion to their suffering comrades. How many times during group sessions have I observed a patient begin to "repent." Such an outpouring often occurs after yet another relapse, when an addict experiences severe emotional pain.

"I lied, stole, hassled to buy a bag . . ." Listening to these confessions, I sometimes wanted to exclaim angrily, as if I were a judge "So, you picked up again! How dare you!"

But patients are not like judges. They know perfectly well that the man is in real trouble. He feels cut off from the world, like an outcast, with no chance to return. Probably this clinic is one glimmer of hope for him to believe that he may not have been "thrown overboard" yet. He won't be condemned here but instead reassured. I do not exaggerate when I say that drug addicts and alcoholics know how to forgive and sympathize with each other at the highest level of humanity. This is the real miracle for me to witness—this moment when users with deep compassion and forgiveness resuscitate a hopeless addict back to life. I have rarely come across such miraculous mercy in any other place as I have in drug treatment clinics.

Are drug addicts the greatest humanitarians? Is this a joke?

No, it is true. No one is capable of being more humane to a drug addict during a breakdown than a fellow addict.

They would probably be saints, except for one critical point:

They can empathize deeply, but only with and for each other. For strangers, for so-called "normal people," the addicts' hearts are often closed, with rarely a drop of sympathy.

Sometimes, though rarely, even the most seasoned addict cannot determine who stands before him: one of his own kind or the other? An addict or not?

That's how it was with Kevin. No one could discover which one he was. He neither distanced himself from the group of students nor merged with it. He was neither ours nor theirs. Not with us, not with them. Decide for yourself. Better yet—don't worry about Kevin. Just mind yourself.

At the graduation ceremony, all of the graduates were expected to give a small speech. Kevin's presentation was awaited with great anticipation. We all knew he was a man of few words. But his apt comments, sharp cutting humor, and unexpected outbursts of laughter suggested that a different man was hidden inside. We hoped Kevin would finally remove the mask and reveal himself.

On the eve of the ceremony, the excitement and curiosity around Kevin swelled. The Riddle of this Sphinx must be solved! Heated debates took place during the break. The majority was of the view that Kevin was one of "ours."

Who was right?

After receiving his diploma, Kevin offered a short speech. He thanked the teachers and wished success to all his classmates. And then, to everyone's dismay, he fell silent.

"Ke-vin, Ke-vin, Ke-vin . . ." one of the students began to call out Kevin's name, rhythmically pounding his hand on the desk.

Others joined in. Within a minute, all students in the auditorium were drumming in unison on the desks.

"Ke-vin! Ke-vin!"

He was taken aback. He looked around as if searching for an escape path.

"Ke-vin!! Ke-vin!!!" thundered the audience.

Kevin blinked several times, then, head bowed low, uttered: "Yes."

"Kevin! Why were you silent this whole time?! Why did you torture yourself and us?! Brother!"

STRANGE VISIONS

"LOOK AT THE TRASHCAN!"

Gradually, I got used to my studies. Month after month was passing by. After classes, I took a subway from Queens to Manhattan in order to "make hours" working as a security guard in the supermarket of the Time Warner building.

If you want to know what my job entailed, I'll tell you in a few words. During my eight-hour shift, I was standing next to the high trashcan. Upon the decision of my supervisor, I should hence and forever have the post on the first floor of the supermarket, near the escalator next to the trash bin. My assignment was to watch out and protect. To watch out that the trash bin didn't overflow and, if it did happen, to report it promptly to the supervisor. To watch out for emergencies—swearing, falls, fighting customers on the floor. To look for suspicious persons—possible shoplifters. But the main task, however, as my supervisor constantly reminded me, was to keep an eye on the trashcan.

I stood, shifting from foot to foot. During this time, I either thought about tomorrow's exam at school or quietly sang my favorite songs. "Oh Lord, won't you buy me a Mercedes Benz?"

The first two or three hours of the shift were spent with such thoughts and singing. Towards the fourth hour, my mood was getting seemingly worse, with no desire to sing anything. The last couple of hours of the shift were deathly torture. My legs felt as though they were made of steel from the long hours of standing in the same spot. My back ached.

"Oh Lord, why are You so cruel to me?!"

THE SCARECROW IN FRONT OF THE UNIVERSITY

Not far from the Time Warner building is the Church of St. Paul the Apostle. I went there during lunch often, turning off my annoying walkie-talkie.

It was solemnly quiet. I came up to the white marble bowl in the center, towering above a small marble sculpture of the Apostle Paul. I dipped the fingers of my right hand into the bowl with warm water and then brought the wet fingers to my forehead, touched my eyes and lips. Thin, warm streams ran down my face, dripping on the gray uniform jacket. I made the sign of the Cross and sat on the bench as God's grace descended upon my heart.

I looked upon the high altar, at the sculptures and icons, at the face of Christ, and at the Apostles. And my life already did not seem so horrible, dumb, and meaningless. I believed once again that—in my arrival to America, in my strange-at-first-glance choice of career to help drug addicts, and even the dumb and exhausting work as a security guard at this place—there is some meaning, that God in spite of everything leads me down a mysterious road, to some grand goal, even though I can't yet understand what this goal entails.

"Okay, if I can't understand now, I could later. Sooner or later everything will be revealed; everything secret becomes apparent," I convinced myself. "I must stick to this path, no matter how hard it may be. While you take the reins, you should not look back."

Sometimes the organ would sound in the church as the musician performed religious pieces. The Church chorales sounded triumphant under the arches of this wonderful church proclaiming the greatness and power of God, the beauty of life, and the belief that Beauty and Goodness are eternal.

Students passed by the Time Warner building day and night. Guys and gals a bit younger than me, with bags containing textbooks and laptops, walked in small groups or by themselves. Some of them were in a hurry, it seems, being late for class, while some walked unhurriedly, talking loudly amongst themselves. A student is easily recognizable, no matter what country, age, sex, or race.

Sometimes I guarded the entrance to the underground garage in the supermarket. I stood by the wide entry in my cap and wrinkled uniform, which was a size too large for me. From the side, I probably looked like my favorite character from the famous story "Wizard of Oz," the straw man called Scarecrow.

Once, overtaken by curiosity, I decided to track where these students went to study, which college. Leaving my post in the garage, I followed them and soon found myself by the beautiful building of Fordham University.

I did not know anything about this University then. This building was located across the street from the Church of St. Paul the Apostle, but I had never paid attention to the university's building.

I stood for a few minutes in front of this building, examining its beautiful glass facade and the students and teachers who came through its doors. The weather was wonderful, and I didn't want to leave.

To the right of the square at the entrance, birch trees grew, and under their canopy stood a bronze sculpture of some saint in a torn frock. I went there and sat down on the granite slab. Turning my face towards the gentle sun rays, I closed my eyes. I listened to the chirping of birds on the birch branches and the roar of the cars passing by. The bell rang in the Church of St. Paul the Apostle.

Ding… Dong—a deep, powerful boom rang through the air, muffling all the other sounds.

Suddenly some strange visions began to appear before me. It was as if I saw my future: myself as a student of this university, my future wife, and my own daughter. I saw myself, in a white lab coat, in the emergency department of some hospital, saving a patient from a drug overdose. These visions made me feel a bit dizzy, and I lost track of time.

Ding… Dong—rang the bell.

Suddenly my walkie-talkie squealed, returning me to reality. It was my shift supervisor at Time Warner asking where I was and why had I left the post and what was the situation on the floor.

I squeezed the walkie-talkie in my hand. Such anger seized me that I could hardly resist throwing the damn radio on the ground and breaking it.

"God damn him and his f..king trashcan!" I got up and trudged back to the supermarket, to my post.

SCHOOL IS OUT—INTO THE WORLD!

I was about to write a cliché—"time flies"—and my hand held still for a moment. A year went by. That is true, but did it really fly by, without me noticing?

How could I forget the bumpy subway cars I had to travel on from one end of the city in Brooklyn to another (to the school in Queens), then to the Time Warner building in Manhattan, and at midnight back home to Brooklyn? Some days I spent around five hours per day commuting on the subway.

In between classes and work, I had to carve out time to read textbooks and lecture notes, complete homework, and prep for exams.

Where to find the time to think, to ponder all that was new and never-before-encountered? To find answers to the billions of questions, beginning from the simplest: how do you smoke this goddamn crack? What does it look like? Like a powder? No, they say it looks like little rocks. The later questions are more complex and difficult: Who are these people, these drug users? They have the same arms, legs, and heads as others do. But there's something unusual, something about them.

Of course, more than once I asked myself: Did I make the right choice? Was it a mistake to believe my "dear aunt" when she said, "What could be easier than becoming a substance abuse counselor?" Wouldn't it have been better to choose something more peaceful, more intellectual? Maybe work as a teacher or librarian? The doubts began to grow, in hundreds of voices—some gentle, some demanding—repeating, "Leave, drop out!" Then I would remember the pledge I made to myself: that I was going to see at least one endeavor to the end.

Yes, I worked hard for this diploma. Over the course of a year, I didn't read one leisurely novel, only textbooks. Goodbye, great literature and philosophy, Shakespeare and Tolstoy, Hemingway and Fitzgerald. Goodbye! Hello, heroin, cocaine, and methadone! Hello, rehabs and detoxes! Good day, parole and probation officers! "You shoot dope and snort coke." I knew this by heart now. I got an "A" on the test. Thanks, Peter, my American brother! Thank you!

Whatever effort it took for me to receive the prized diploma, it paled in comparison with—and I am not afraid to use the term—the Herculean labor my fellow students spent for the same purpose. My classmates, who killed their mind, body, and soul with alcohol and junk for ten, fifteen years in a row. Some of them did not live at home, surrounded by loved ones, but in halfway houses, where there was often fighting and theft. After classes, I went to work or home, but they had to go to a clinic to continue their treatment. Among those who made it through, several were still on parole or probation or involved in different courts.

All of them were still "raw," not only professionally but psychologically. The majority continued their old patterns: they quarreled often and went into hysterics or anger at the slightest provocation. There were those who went to the dean to snitch on their classmates or teachers and those who flirted. The instance with Sylvia speaks for itself, where a honeymoon for two ended in relapse and expulsion of both love birds from school.

About a third of them—seven out of twenty—were unable to finish school. They mysteriously vanished, or—simply put—they fell off the wagon. And not for a day or two, but to the point that they forgot they were even enrolled in school.

Yet these "damaged outcasts" suddenly found the inner strength to raise themselves. They attended classes, did their homework, and passed exams for a whole year. Unthinkable! Many could not believe what they themselves had accomplished.

And tomorrow they appear in the clinics and hospitals of New York, not to be treated but to treat active[2] addicts and alcoholics. *They* were supposed to do this. *They?!*

Graduation was an unforgettable sunny day. The whole classroom was decorated with flowers and balloons. The graduating students were in suits and nice dresses, and everyone was spotlessly clean, fragrant with perfume and cologne. There was endless patting of shoulders; there were jokes and there was laughter.

Alas, not that many spouses were in attendance. Mostly siblings and friends. Of course, teachers, administrators, and the director all came as well. They handed out the diplomas. Each graduating student gave a little speech as a farewell and thank you. Many began to cry before they could finish. No one was able to conceal their feelings. As I would later come to understand, with all their mastery of false facades and manipulation, addicts are unable to deal with emotions, especially positive ones that they're so unfamiliar with.

Mrs. Terri handed me my diploma. She was the administrative assistant director, the same one who asked me a year earlier "why are you going into this field?" and warned me strictly about drug use on the premises. The students liked her and treated her with respect. They felt that Terri understood them, and forgave her strict approach, as they themselves knew that they needed this discipline and could not be left to their own devices. During the ceremony, students gave her a lot of flowers.

Barbara was one of the last students after me to take the microphone. She was a short, stout Puerto Rican woman. She didn't stand out throughout the whole school year, didn't say much, and preferred to stay in the shadows. She hadn't been a drug user, but because she had been in prison the students considered her one of their own. Barbara particularly did not like to share and didn't make public declarations of dramatic stories from her life. The group did not have that much interest in her.

When she took the microphone, many faces expressed "What a bore!" Now they would have to listen to this boring Barbara, who likely would not sob or sing or run out of the auditorium in tears. It would be better if she refused to talk at all.

Barbara was quiet for a moment, looking through the window. Then she began to speak quietly, pacing thoughtfully throughout the auditorium.

"My husband was a drug dealer. He sold a lot of drugs, and I helped him. My husband was shot and I picked up his business." As she spoke, Barbara continued to walk slowly from one side of the auditorium to another, staring ahead as if she did not see the flowers or the shiny balloons. "The FBI busted me. They confiscated all the cocaine and methadone I was selling. The prosecutor asked for the maximum: twenty-five years by the Rockefeller drug laws, but the judge took pity on me and gave me fifteen without the right for parole." She kept pacing, and her speech floated through the hushed, somewhat startled auditorium. "I was angry, despite the judge giving me such a lenient sentence. I started selling drugs in prison. I saw how people were killed over drugs and some died from overdoses, but I didn't care. I didn't use myself. I shot dope a couple of times out of curiosity, and I smoked pot rarely. One day they tested me for HIV and it came out positive. I went to the prison yard and sat there for a long time. I understood that this was God's punishment for all the evil I had inflicted on others. I decided to kill myself. The day I was going to carry out my plan, they called me to the medical unit and repeated the test. It turned out I was negative! There was an error. They'd just mixed up my prison number with another woman. Since then, I ask God for forgiveness every day."

Barbara kept slowly pacing from one wall to another, probably as she had done in her cell for fifteen years in prison.

"Next week, I'll be working at the probation office as a volunteer. I'll make copies and do filing. During the interview, someone called the officer, and he left for a short while, leaving me alone in the office. His cloak hung on a coat rack. He trusted me. A Probation officer trusted me. Me?! When I got home, I told this to my mother. She held me tightly and said that God is returning me to His grace."

When Barbara finished, the auditorium was completely silent for a long time—for the first time in the entire, long academic year. Faces were pensive and gloomy. Each recognized his own life, in one way or another, in Barbara's story.

At the end of the ceremony, assistant director Terri took a stand.

"You're needed there!" She pointed to somewhere outside the window of the classroom. "People need you out there! They're waiting for you! You know how much they need you there!" Terri said loudly.

The students listened to her speech with full attentiveness. Perhaps it was the first time in many years they didn't feel themselves as outcasts, as garbage, as thieves or prostitutes. They saw themselves not even as graduating students, but as missionaries who would soon have to fulfill an extraordinarily difficult and often thankless mission.

Then Terri began to pick flowers from her bouquet and gave them out to each of us.

MY DEAR AUNT

"So, you graduated from school? Became a cool pro?" she asked.

"Yes, I'm done with school and got a diploma," I answered. "I wouldn't say I am pro just yet."

"Then let's drink to you becoming the best substance abuse counselor in New York!" She elegantly raised her glass of warm sake.

"Okay." I supported her toast, raising my glass.

With my "dear aunt" in a sushi bar, we kept toasting my diploma.

She was about forty-five. She sat across from me at a table in a light-colored, décolleté dress, with beads on her tanned chest.

"You'll be a good counselor, I'm sure. You are interested in people; you are not indifferent to them," she said.

"Good to hear this, thanks. You've helped me like an angel. But how can I get a job in my new profession? Everywhere they require experience. Tell me, how do I get this goddamn experience? I still work as a security guard, guarding that fucking trashcan every day!"

The sushi boat suddenly appeared on the table, thanks to the waitress. It held a variety of rolls and sashimi.

"Is your resume done already?" she asked.

"Yes, of course."

"Do you want my help with getting a job? There are no openings now in my clinic. But I know the manager in another outpatient clinic. I could ask him to talk to their director."

"Sure thing, do it. If I get a job, then I'll owe you another sushi feast."

We had more sake. My dear aunt taught me how to use chopsticks instead of a fork. Sake warmed us on the inside, and on the deck of the food boat, there were fewer and fewer rice balls and salmon pieces.

The waiter brought the check. I paid for our fine dinner, while my aunt added ten bucks for the tip.

We left the bar when it was already dark. Slowly we went to the subway down the square. We were both feeling loose and relaxed on this warm autumn evening.

"Oh, Peter, it's so nice being with you, a real feast for the soul!" she said, taking my arm. She pressed her breast against my shoulder.

It occurred to me that she might want to continue the "soul feast" at my house.

"I want to tell you something about your angel. I am going through a hard time now; I am divorcing from my husband." She kept silent for a while. "While I was going to meet with you today, I was thinking whether or not to sleep with you. I assumed I would feel better then. I feel ashamed to reveal this. So silly, isn't it? Please, forget what I just said."

She suddenly stopped and, embracing my head, lifted herself to her tiptoes and kissed me on the lips. "Thank you, Pete."

"For what?'

"Just for an amazing evening. I'll help you get a very good job."

PART TWO

THE FIRST JOB: "WHAT AM I DOING HERE?"

The outpatient clinic where I landed a job was not in a prestigious neighborhood in Brooklyn, but it also wasn't in a dangerous area.

The director was an Italian woman named Francesca, about forty-five years old, not very tall and well-proportioned. She had a gift of winning a person over and creating a pleasant conversational atmosphere. She had a charming smile. But she could also be rude and abrasive.

Unfortunately, I was paid only $15.00 an hour, the same as at my security job at the Time Warner building. Or, rather, fifty cents less. Thank you, dear aunt, for getting me such a good job.

That's okay, I consoled myself. As we say in America, the key is to get your foot in the door. To take that first step, and then . . . prospects, career, and of course, money.

The clinic, uncharted territory for me, dealt with a specific population. Patients there were not working people. They weren't college students, and they weren't writers or musicians. The patients were, in general, sent there for treatment by the court, many released from jail. They were either on parole or probation in exchange for agreeing to receive substance abuse treatment.

From eight-thirty in the morning until nine at night, there

was a nonstop stream of people, right up until the clinic doors closed.

The bosses of the clinic had recently opened two sober houses: two small buildings situated in a high-crime section of East New York, each designed to house a hundred people. This was supposed to be a place for those who had nowhere to go after leaving prison, for those who had no family waiting for them.

At eight-thirty o'clock sharp each morning, several vans loaded with patients would arrive at the building. The patients were delivered to the clinic and then returned to the sober houses after several group sessions. Then the vans would return to the clinic with another set of patients. This pipeline to and fro operated at maximum efficiency: there was not one free seat either in the vehicles or in the rooms where the sessions took place.

Young female receptionists sat in the registration office, continuously adding checkmarks to the patients' account forms. The counselors were endlessly signing their names below each checkmark. Accountants would then send the claims to Medicaid.

The little clinic buzzed like a beehive: *bzzz . . . bzzz . . .*

Then, there were new patients who had just been released from prison, sitting in the waiting area, their backpacks and old wheeled suitcases in hand. Some were already high, having met up with their drug man on the way here.

Bzzz . . . bzzz . . .

Oh, my dreams from a year ago that excited my imagination, where are you now? When I entered the substance abuse school, I assumed that in the near future I would meet artists and rock stars suffering from drug dependency. But I now recalled my fellow students from the drug Institute with some sadness. Why had I so hastily taken them to be hooligans, street thugs, and criminals? My dear classmates—where are you? How was I, an ignoramus, unable to evaluate your merits? Now it seems you were the best of the best, the most capable and persistent, having made the climb to the first rung out of this filth!

All of the current patients merged into one blurry face, regardless of race and nationality. There were African Americans, Whites, and Hispanics, but they all resembled one another. Was it their humble clothing? Their coarse faces? Their poor manners? Their hoarse, slurred voices?

I wasn't struck so much by their bad manners or outward appearance, the stab wounds and prison tattoos, as by the content that came out of their mouths. Not one of them provoked violence or threatened anyone. Far from it. Rather, their talk resembled that of philosophers and thinkers.

True, in the heat of an argument, they could sometimes swear roughly, no matter how insistent I was that they be careful with their F-words. Yet how sensibly they speculated about life! They talked about how it was so necessary to manage one's emotions and listen to the voice of reason, to have faith in God, and to live in harmony with oneself and others. To overlook the faults of others and work hard to overcome one's own. To refrain from worrying too much about the future and not dwell on the past. To live one day at a time!

And most important of all, as they all said in unison and individually: *"Don't use drugs or alcohol! It's so evil! This damn heroin, crack, grass, vodka. If it weren't for the drugs, my wife and I never would have divorced; I wouldn't have lost my job or gone to prison. I would have a family, a job, an apartment, a car. I would be someone. And what am I now? I am nothing. Fucking junkie! I live in a sober house. I need to report to my parole officer once a week. I have to take urine tests everywhere I go. I'm on food stamps. And why all of this? Because of coke and booze. But now I'm serious about being on the road to recovery. I'm going to be careful, listen to the voice of reason, and live in harmony."*

Just about everything they said was in that spirit.[3]

"What am I doing here?" I asked myself as I listened to these people. I expected to be teaching them about how bad it is to use drugs and alcohol. And here they were, saying the same, knowing better than I did how bad it is!

But how did such deeply thoughtful people wind up in prison? How could they condemn drugs so zealously, yet still use them for years? How was it possible to reconcile their speech, full of humanistic pathos, with their criminal offenses and angry faces?

There was another question I couldn't answer: Where did all these people disappear to, and why? They are under the supervision of the court! Those who drop out of treatment face the risk of returning to prison. What are they doing? Again wandering the city—again snorting, smoking, stealing, and robbing? Just yesterday they were here at this very spot, talking so wisely about the dangers of drugs. Had they all lied? Were they pretending?

Questions, questions . . .

LIZA: THE SWEET LADY THAT COULD

We shared an office together.

Her parents had come from Sicily many years ago, and Liza was born in America. She was olive-skinned, with thick black hair like crow's wings, large dark-brown eyes, and sensual lips that she painted with bright lipstick. Her makeup, though also bright, was well matched. Liza's manner of dress emulated a fashionable socialite, though she never achieved that level, as there was also something vulgar about her.

She had a booming voice and loud laughter. Even at sixty-three years old, she could still get away with dressing sexy, appearing in a low-cut dress that showcased her breasts.

Liza had a hot temper and it was extremely difficult for her to sit for a long time in one spot and stay quiet. She was always being carried away somewhere, and she was overwhelmed by the thirst for activity. The thirst for conversation. The thirst for revelation.

I had only worked at the clinic for just a week and already knew a lot about Liza. I had gotten this knowledge directly from her. If I didn't know something, it was only because we didn't have much free time to talk. Moreover, Francesca the director frowned upon personal conversations between coworkers. Francesca had a strange habit of walking through the corridors and peeking through the little window in the doors to see how the treatment was going. She lost her composure when a counselor was sitting in his office alone without a patient. How can the billing department make a claim to Medicaid? Hey, counselor: No sitting alone—grab any patient and get him into the office!

This is what I learned about Liza. When her parents arrived in New York, they opened a small pizzeria, working there night and day to feed their children and provide them with a decent education. Her parents saved money for their children to go to college. Liza started using drugs when she was fifteen and barely graduated from high school. On more than one occasion, her parents had to post bail and pay a lawyer to get her out of jail. I don't recall if she told me the exact number of times she had been arrested or how long she had been imprisoned, but it was definitely more than once. According to Liza, the last time she was arrested was two years earlier, right in the clinic where she worked. They took her out of the office in handcuffs and brought her straight to the police station. That arrest was on prior charges: there was a warrant for her arrest and the police caught up with her many years later.

For the most part, Liza's arrests and jail time were for drug possession. (This is a neat trick the System has devised: the criminal offense is not for use, but for possession. But is it really possible to use drugs without having them?)

However, Liza also had a criminal record for burglaries in which she had participated with her ex-husband, a man who was apparently a great adventurer. He involved his wife in all kinds of criminal exploits. Somehow, they managed to have two kids in between the arrests and hospital detox stays. By the time Liza and I met, her children were grown up and had families of their own.

Liza's husband died from an overdose, and she herself struggled for a long time with her addiction. She'd get treated, relapsed, get arrested again, get treated again—sometimes mandated and sometimes voluntary. Altogether, this struggle lasted almost twenty-five years—a quarter of a century! Liza worked as a substance abuse counselor for more than fifteen years in numerous clinics. She hadn't worked long at the one where we met, and therefore here she was a newbie, just like me.

We immediately felt a mutual affection. Liza said she liked my "simplicity of heart." She said that even though I was intelligent, not raised on the streets, and had read many books, I wasn't conceited or full of myself.

She told me about her past in a picturesque way, with humor and irony. For instance, there was this story. Liza and her husband had robbed an apartment. He'd climbed in through the window of a four-story building, and she stood on the roof to receive the stolen goods. As this was the winter, it was terribly cold and a snowstorm began. Liza was waiting for her husband for God knows how long, growing numb. She jumped up and down and slapped her arms to keep warm. She couldn't figure out why her husband was taking so long to appear, and why so many police cars with flashing lights were driving up to the building.

It turned out that her hubby had discovered syringes and morphine while rummaging through some drawers. And, of course, he decided to use it right away. He was so high that he didn't notice the owners had come home and called the police.

In describing this event, Liza expressed outrage at her husband's behavior, how rude it was for him to think only about getting high and not about the wife he had left on the roof. More so, she blamed herself and not her husband, and laughed at her gullibility.

Yes, despite her age and experiences, Liza sincerely felt she was a naïve and gullible woman. She believed that this "character defect" was the source of her many problems in life.

In this way, Liza was typical of her peers: Almost all drug users sincerely believe they are naïve and very easily fooled. They claim they have suffered because of their gullibility. But, having suffered much at the hands of others, they've learned that no one in the world is to be trusted.

All people are malicious and cunning and take advantage of the drug user's trust. Doesn't this sound ridiculous? At first, I thought they were kidding. How could someone who has lied incessantly, robbed, broken oaths, spent time in jail—how could such a person be called naïve?

But over time, after constantly hearing similar points of view from different patients, I began to reconsider. Could they be right? They couldn't all be conspiring to proclaim their credulity.

Naiveté and gullibility are not the most precise words to correctly describe a drug user's character. A user's problem is his inability to comprehend the complex nature of human relationships. They understand ways to secure money for drugs and use them, but with relationships at work, with family, or in society, most users behave like teenagers: they either place implicit trust in those who cannot be trusted or else lie to those who take care of their welfare. They see the world as black and white, with few shades of gray, much less the other colors on the palette of complex human interactions. They rush from one extreme to another, express rage at others, and then become angry with themselves. Convoluted and twisted, surrounded by broken relationships, unable to assess their situation calmly and sensibly, they turn vehemently defensive. They convince themselves they are victims and everyone else is the enemy. They begin to battle with the world (with you, dear reader). They come to think, "I've had enough of being a sheep waiting for slaughter. I will be a wolf."

This twisted philosophy makes it very challenging to treat drug addicts. A counselor is faced with two opposite personalities embodied in one—an oversensitive sheep and a heartless wolf. Any strong voice intonation or direct words trigger the sheep, the victim mentality—the addict is easily offended and puts his guard up. By contrast, too soft and sympathetic an approach can provoke the addict's wolf instinct, as he becomes sneaky and angry.

Imagine the challenge of treating someone like that!

Now back to Liza. She told me her parents used to lock her in the house so she couldn't go out with her friends. The temptation of drugs boosted her strength and pushed her to heroic acts: Liza broke the glass windows to jump through them, she sold drugs, and she danced in a strip club. Three times, loan sharks and dealers caught her on the street and put a gun to her head.

As I listened to Liza, I imagined the streets of the New York of her youth, the areas where Italians lived, having arrived half-starved from post-war Sicily. Parents worked long and hard in pizzerias and bakeries, and their children . . . some went to college (like our director Francesca) while others became street urchins and hooligans, swelling the ranks of the well-known New York Italian mafia. Notwithstanding her years and professional achievements, Liza still retained recognizable signs of the "mischievous girl," with prominent battle scars from growing up on the rough streets of New York.

When our mutual trust increased, she showed me the thin white lines on her arms—tracks from abscesses. The same mementos could also be seen, from her ankles to her knees, on her dark, strong legs.

Liza could be very inconsistent in her relations with colleagues. She would see them as true friends, go out to lunch with them, and open up. Then suddenly, unexpectedly, she would change her mind about them and add them to her enemy list.

She was not timid, of course. I remember one evening in the middle of autumn, we had left work at the same time and walked toward the subway. The weather was lousy, with slush and a chill wind. We talked about work and complained about our director Francesca, with whom Liza had begun to clash:

"This isn't a clinic. It's a fucking business," Liza said indignantly. "No one is thinking about the patients. Peter, I know you never got high. But try to put yourself in their shoes. They just got out of prison yesterday. They have no job, no education, no money. They don't have a damn thing! Don't forget they're chronic drug users and alcoholics, and twenty-four hours a day they want to use. They hate everyone and trust no one. But all the same, they have hope. And tell me: How do people at the clinic treat them? Like cattle!"

Next, Liza directed her criticism toward the director, holding her responsible for the terrible state of the clinic. Most of all, she resented Francesca's passion for fashionable clothes. She had a point. "Franchi," as we called her, would often leave during work hours in her sparkling new Jeep and return a couple of hours later carrying huge bags imprinted with designer names. Her expensive wardrobe was in stark contrast to the clothes most of our patients wore.

We turned down a side street to take a shortcut. This was not the best idea. Liza was wearing a red woolen coat that evening and carried a handbag under her arm. In short, she looked like a socialite going to an event.

What happened next, well . . . scenes like this in novels and films haven't made a strong impression on us in a long time—they are too trivial. Who today is interested in reading about a banal street robbery, where some young robber intends to take a woman's purse containing twenty dollars, a subway card, and makeup?

But in this instance, the events unfolded in an unpredictable way. Liza grabbed the purse, which was already in the robber's hands. I instinctually wanted to help but realized Liza didn't need me. She rushed wildly toward the guy and kneed him between the legs. He was taken aback and must have been shocked by the fighting spirit of this respectable lady. Clutching her handbag, Liza not only set her free hand in motion but, even worse, her tongue. She gave him a real verbal lashing; the choice words she unleashed I had not heard even from my roughest patients. Moreover, she took off after him.

Fleeing for secured space, the guy stopped and answered her from a distance, also swearing.

Liza had a ready retort. "Get some treatment, you fucking junkie!" Even in such a situation, she remembered her professional duty.

I considered my American brother, Peter, as my first teacher in the first grade or even kindergarten of my addiction studies. Liza became my second teacher on this difficult subject of substance abuse. She tried to convey information on the subject that wasn't printed in books. Much of what formerly appeared unimportant to me actually deserved special attention. Some things I never even knew existed.

Once, after watching *Goodfellas*, a famous film starring Robert De Niro about the Italian Mafia in America, I asked:

"Why would the Mafia family abandon one of the characters once he started dealing drugs? How is it any worse than racketeering?"

Liza expounded: "The problem isn't that he started to sell, but that he sold heroin specifically, and he began dipping and dabbing."

It turns out that the Italian Mafia holds an extremely negative attitude about heroin. They believe that anyone who touches heroin becomes unreliable and easily breaks with tradition. It is ill-advised to have either a business or a personal relationship with such a person.

"But why heroin in particular?" I asked, perplexed. "What's the difference? Is someone who snorts coke or drinks any more reliable?"

"Pete, what are you talking about? Of course, there's a huge difference!" answered Liza. "The idea of 'your drug of choice' is not for nothing. A person doesn't pick a specific drug by accident."

Having covered the window in the door of our office with a piece of cardboard reading "Session in progress. Don't disturb!" Liza introduced me to the intricacies of this complicated subject, "Your Drug of Choice."

She was a true professor in this area. Of course, a quarter-century of use! Moreover, she was multifaceted: She'd snorted coke, smoked weed, and popped pills. But her true love was heroin.

"Every drug alters your mood in a different way. Tell me what drug you use, and I'll tell you who you are, what kind of person you are," Liza began her lecture. "Let's take cocaine, for instance. It's like you're soaring; you feel like you're on top of the highest mountain. And from there, from the peak, you look below. You're the king of the world! There's nobody higher than you, more powerful or smarter than you are! What do you think of that? Just imagine: A minute ago you were in rags, a pathetic worm. Everything around you was dark and damp. Suddenly the sun rays break through, everything lights up, and you've gone from being a rat in a dirty basement to becoming the Almighty Lord God Himself!" Liza's beautiful dark brown eyes sparkled and a touch of madness flashed briefly across her face.

"Yes, but . . ." I said, wanting to bring Liza back down to the ground. "Heroin? What about that? Doesn't a heroin user have the sensation that he rules the world?"

"Oh, no. Heroin is a very subtle substance. Dope is a secret. It's mystical, a world of half shadows and mysterious whispers." Liza lowered her eyelids and relaxed slowly into her armchair as if she were sinking into an invisible hot tub of bliss. "The dope addict is calm and cool, like a python. He doesn't hurry or jolt himself into the clouds. The dope addict's whole being gets into the high, into all its nooks and crannies, and he relishes and captures every nuance of it."

In her black pantsuit, Liza began to make slow, swimming movements; she wriggled her hands, and her whole body squirmed. She resembled a soulless snake. Or rather, the soul of this snake was heroin.

"The heroin addict is cleverer and craftier than the cocaine addict. He's secretive, and all his senses are buried in the deepest hiding places. He calculates carefully; he is a psychologist of the highest order. But he knows the prize: dope lowers you into such blissful warmth, enveloping your entire body and soul so that you'd give everything on the earth if you could only stay there and not return to this cold world. Understanding the heroin addict, Pete, is not that simple. It takes a lot of time."

"And an alcoholic? Does alcohol really work differently? Alcohol also submerges you, warms you up. It even burns your throat and stomach," I countered, not taking my eyes off Liza, who continued to flutter about on warm waves.

Liza finally shook off the intoxicating daydream that had pulled her for a short time into the distant past. Hearing about alcohol—after heroin—she looked at me with pity as if to say, "Poor guy, he knows nothing about life."

"Is it really possible to compare alcohol with heroin? Pete, what are you talking about?! Why did they give you a substance abuse certificate? Alcohol is hogwash that destroys the mind and body. Of course, I also drank to help with dope withdrawal or just to be buzzed. But what is an alcoholic? He gets ten-fifteen bucks, goes to the store, buys a pint of booze, and drinks at home. He cries about his unhappy life and collapses into sleep. He is pathetic. No offense, dear. I know that you Russians have a special love for alcohol. Mother Russia, glug, glug!" She formed her fingers around an imaginary bottle and lifted it to her open mouth. Then she squished her face up humorously as if she had just downed a bottle of bitter vodka.

We both laughed.

In addition to the patients who were mandated for treatment, several "volunteers," those who came of their own volition, attended the clinic. Among these were a handful of seniors: three men of about sixty-five years of age. One was Italian, another Puerto Rican, and the third Jewish. It was amazing how they had managed to live to such an age. Active drug users rarely make it to fifty years old. They die from an overdose, cardiac arrest, or a blood infection, or from bullets and accidents they had while they were intoxicated. But this "trinity" had miraculously survived. Two of them had been friends since their youth, beginning back in the glorious 1970s.

All three, of course, looked like old men, sick and tormented. Sometimes I would see one of them hobbling along the corridor with a cane. I'd wave to him in greeting and go to my office. I'd make a couple of phone calls, write progress notes on a patient's chart, exchange a few words with Liza, come out of my office, and that same patient would still be in the corridor, having made it only halfway down the hall. It was difficult for him to move with swollen legs and a belly distended from cirrhosis of the liver. And he had no strength in his arms.

Sometimes the three men would gather with Liza and me in the office, have a little get-together, and recall yesteryear. We were not their primary counselors, but they liked our office where, instead of the typical posters about the benefits of sobriety, there hung still life and landscape prints along with religious-themed pictures of a souvenir style that Liza had brought from home. This type of art lifted her spirits.

These three did not come, of course, to admire the pictures, but Liza. Their age united them, or it was a common destiny. They were all veterans from the addiction battlefield, fighters from a drug war that struck down thousands of their peers. The majority of their comrades already lay in their graves, while these three were survivors. For the young twenty-something drug users in the clinic who bought psychotropic pills online, these three were relics of an ancient era. By then, Liza and I had made a new sign: "Session in progress. Don't disturb!" The cardboard covered the glass window in the door without leaving even a tiny crack to see through.

When our "dear guests" arrived, I hung the sign on the door, and Liza, as the friendly hostess, put a tin of cookies on the table. They sat in a circle and started to talk. One would usually begin by complaining about his health. The others would sympathize. Gradually the conversation turned to different topics. Liza sometimes forgot that she was a counselor, not their "comrade." The guests plunged into memories. My God, what memories these were! And recalled with the minutest details.

Wanting to enlighten me, the young clinician that I was, they recommended I read "the greatest book of all time"—*Junkie*, by William S. Burroughs.

In the 1950-60s, this short paperback made a big splash, triggering a strong reaction from American readers and even from the U.S. government. Nowadays, such a book would likely go unnoticed, having no particular artistic merit. However, at that time, it bravely charted new territory. It's a story about the daily life of a New York drug user and how he shot morphine, smoked weed, forged prescriptions, deceived doctors, stole money from subway riders, and "pushed junk." The author wrote from personal experience. Burroughs almost never attempted to sort out the heart of his characters in his book, though he detailed descriptions of getting high and coming down, and on the acquisition and technical aspects of using junk.

I criticized the work for its artistic shortcomings, but the "comrades" were appalled by the nonsense I spouted.

"Man, there is not a single mistake in how to use junk in this book! Do you remember how the main character chewed the ashes from his opium cigarette and then washed them down with hot coffee?"

"No, not really."

"Peter, buddy, this means you've understood nothing in this book! Or maybe you read Tolstoy's *War and Peace* by accident instead of *Junkie*?"

The homemade D. I. Y. syringes from eye droppers, the chewing of opium ash—today, this sounds comparable to the stories of ancient people making stone axes. But for these three old-timers, this was their youth, their life.

In the long-gone fifties and sixties, drug addiction in the United States was considered not a disease, but a crime. Drug users were not engaged with doctors, but mainly with the police and the courts. Drug users in withdrawal at special medical stations were given weak sedatives or aspirin-like painkillers, and they were allowed to shower. The treatment ended there. Or they were sent to a psych ward where they would be strapped to the bed. But more often, they were still driven to the police station and, from there, to court.

Eventually, the first specialized drug addiction clinics began to appear. There was a new realization that substance abuse is a disease and it needs to be treated as a disease. The first drug addiction clinics began to appear. The measures taken to treat patients in those first rehab clinics were, by today's standards, draconian and resembled those used in prisons. Group therapy was more like emotional lynching. Nevertheless, this was a tremendous breakthrough in the treatment of substance abuse.[4]

The Burroughs book made an invaluable contribution to this movement. This book opened the eyes of many to the fact that a drug user has his attachments, his friends, and his loves. He is still a human being.

I loved when Liza prayed. Liza grew up in a devout Catholic family. By her own admission, she had only really turned to religion when she began to fight with addiction. She said that without the Church, without God, she wouldn't have pulled through.

This was true—her emotional state was very rocky. Poor Liza was often anxious about little things, would get easily irritated, and erupt in anger both toward her patients and colleagues. Her friends and enemies would often swap status. Sometimes she would lock herself in our office and cry. She would weep like a child whose feelings had been hurt, and I felt much pity for her at those times. Having observed her, I concluded that, without some deep inner foundation, Liza would not keep her balance. She would have broken down and spiraled into the abyss if she hadn't taken up God.

When she was at the edge, about to lose her equilibrium, like a drowning person clutching at straws, then Liza would hang on to prayer.

"Oh, it's all nonsense. They're not worth my worry. I've been cursing too much lately. I get angry and cry a lot. That's dangerous. It's a sin. Kid, let's pray together. It would be good for you, too."

Liza knew that I was an Orthodox Christian and our prayers were similar, even though the languages were different. She slid her office chair towards me and took my hands in hers. She bowed her raven-haired head. I lowered my head as well so that our foreheads were almost touching.

"If you want, repeat after me. You can pray in Russian. The key is to pray." She became very serious.

At other times and under different circumstances, I most likely would not have related to these prayers seriously, feeling instead like a spectator at a play. But my life had changed. As a counselor, every day I encountered something new and frightening. Unanswered questions started to torment me increasingly. My faith in justice was beginning to waver. I didn't know who was to blame for this nightmare, this ugliness and distortion of any truth. God or man?

"Our Father who art in heaven . . ." Liza began with a voice that spoke from deep within her chest, not loudly but with each word carefully intoned.

We prayed together. Blessed warmth emanated from Liza's hands and from her forehead. I swear I felt this heat! I remember it even now.

We prayed for ourselves, for all our relatives, and for all the patients. We clasped each other's hands tightly:

"God, grant me the serenity to accept the things I cannot change. . . Thank you, Lord, for everything . . ."

DON'T BELIEVE YOUR LYING EYES!

In addition to conducting psychotherapy sessions, each counselor in the clinic does intakes for new patients. Here is how that works.

I invited a new patient who sits in the waiting room into my office. He typically comes in carrying some old bags. This signals that he has just been released from prison, is on parole, has been sent for mandated treatment, and has no place to live. He has no money and no job, and his family and friends have refused him. All he has is a list of his convictions and an old sack with his belongings—all of his earthly possessions. Downstairs, outside the clinic building, a van is already waiting to take the new guy to a sober house.

I interviewed the patient using a questionnaire: What is your drug of choice? What education do you have? Have you ever worked? and so on. Then I walk with him to the restroom for the toxicology test. Meanwhile, in the waiting room, a newly arrived patient is already drumming his fingers impatiently on his knees.

The responses to the education question provoked my genuine surprise. The vast majority of patients, regardless of skin color, do not have high school diplomas. How is that possible? In the "capital of the world"? At first, I was surprised when a patient said he had only finished tenth or eleventh grade. After some time, any patient with a high school diploma or GED would surprise me and earn my admiration: "Good job! That's great you were able to graduate from high school!" And if I met someone who had attended a semester or two of college, he would be considered an Einstein!

Still, education—or rather, its lack—was not the most significant of my discoveries.

It was an endless stream of sorrow. The grief that does not scream, or cry, or go into hysterics. This was a sorrow of a different order. It wore a severe, scarred face, with broken and decaying teeth; it had tattooed arms cut by knives and a body bearing gunshot wounds. It had been torn from all family relations. It had endless arrests for robbery, burglary, and selling drugs. It was devoid of real careers or work experience. It was chronically diseased.

I felt sympathy for these first patients: everything in their lives was broken and mangled, and devoid of even a gleam of hope. I listened to them carefully, promised to call somewhere, find something out. But the stream of sorrow would not cease. From all the state prisons, the courts, the detoxes and psychiatric wards, people would arrive at the clinic with their worn baggage.

The mountain of incomplete paperwork grew ominously on my desk. One patient after another sat before me. Their names and faces started to blur in my memory.

"Which drug did you use?"

"Cocaine."

"And marijuana?"

"Yes, weed, too."

"Did you drink?"

"Yes."

"What kind of medical problems do you have?"

"Hypertension, I guess."

"Education?"

"Eleventh grade."

"Any relatives?"

"An ex-wife and daughter. We haven't talked in years."

"What were you convicted of?"

"Robbery."

"And drug possession?"

"Yes, and drug possession."

"Profession?"

"None."

Move quickly, at a gallop—question, answer, x-marks, check marks in empty boxes. No time to look into their eyes.

It often seemed to me at such times that this was not me, but someone else who looked like me, sitting in that office behind the desk and posing question after question to ever-changing faces before him.

The process invaded my dreams. Each night I saw a medley of moving gray figures pacing the clinic halls, mumbling. Suddenly, my voice thundered through the indistinct whispers: "Let's go to take your urine, sir!" These were my first dreams in English.

I will describe the toxicology test in more detail later on. Such an unusual adventure, it deserves a chapter of its own. In the meantime, I will tell how this took place in the clinic and why the phrase "Let's go to take your urine, sir" permeated my dreams.

A patient in the restroom hands a cup of his urine to the counselor. The counselor dips in a white plastic stick with an indicator scale for different drugs. If the urine is "dirty," after a minute or two a red stripe appears across from the name of the specific drug. Will it be positive or negative? Clean or dirty?

On this thin red stripe depends . . . oh, how much depends on this line, you cannot even imagine. One's whole future depends on it. Tomorrow. No, even today!

The clinic rules are very strict. A "dirty" patient will be

thrown out of the sober house immediately. He certainly has nowhere else to live but a filthy shelter or on the street. The counselor from our clinic calls the parole or probation officers to let them know that the patient was using, and then the patient is threatened with prison as a result.

What shocked me, however, was not that prison does not stop them or that their drug use contradicts their philosophical speeches on the benefits of sobriety. I was struck most by how practically all of them assured me—and one another—that they were clean. Without batting an eyelash or flinching a facial muscle, they would say:

"Yes, doctor. I already forgot how to snort goddamn coke. I don't even want to remember this!"

Then we'd walk to the restroom and . . .

The first time I didn't believe my eyes. Why was there a red line?

"Sir, you have a positive result for cocaine."

"Really, doc? Impossible!"

I would take a new test stick and again dip it into the cup. Maybe there had been a technical error? Perhaps it was a bad test stick?

The patient stood by and watched pensively as another red stripe slowly appeared.

I raised my brows.

"Sir, you still have a positive result for cocaine."

"C'mon, doc! Really? No way . . . "

In short, a stream of grief merged with a stream of lies.

I already knew I shouldn't believe what I was hearing. Ears are unreliable instruments for ascertaining honesty. The tongue is also a very doubtful means. Words mean nothing and aren't worth a penny.

I can only believe what I see with my own eyes. The test stick tells the truth. To me, a red line means that trust is lost. This man has no future. The only road for him leads to prison.

If the red line doesn't appear, the man is clean. His conscience is clean. His eyes are clear. I can trust him. Today.

But what about tomorrow?

In my new vision, the thin red line separates the world into two: the clean and the dirty, the positive and the negative, those who have a future and those who do not.

VETERAN ADAM: WAR THAT NEVER ENDS

Adam was a thin, tall, Jewish man with a thick head of graying hair, combed back. He often smiled, but his smile had a tone of "Jewish sadness."

Every morning he brought a hot-off-the-press *New York Times* and *Wall Street Journal*. His reading interests were wide: U.S. foreign and domestic policy, local events, and sports.

His grandfathers and grandmothers, a hundred years ago, immigrated to the States from the Jewish shtetls of Poland and Hungary and brought up their children in the traditions of pre-war Eastern European Jews. Adam's parents preserved many of the traditions of their ancestors and placed their only son in a yeshiva. Adam graduated from the yeshiva, but did not become religious; he attended synagogue only on major Jewish holidays.

Adam was a Vietnam War veteran. Here is the story of how he found himself serving in the U. S. Army.

Adam was in college. He studied poorly because of "sex, drugs, and rock 'n' roll." One day, a side job turned up for him and his buddy; they had earned some money and decided to "have a little fun" with drinking, swallowing LSD, and hanging out in the famous Astroland Amusement Park in Brooklyn.

Not far from the entrance to the park was an army recruitment booth. The Vietnam war was underway at that time. For fun, these cheerful friends entered the booth and asked how they could become defenders of the Motherland. They were told: "You guys need to be physically fit and willing to serve in the Army. That's it." The boys laughed and said that they were conscientious pacifists and against any war. They went to the park to enjoy the carousel. "Enjoy the rides, kids."

Continuing the festivities, they bought more whiskey and LSD. While very high, they decided they were ready to defend America from all its enemies. Once again, they entered that wonderful recruitment booth, showed their driver's licenses, filled out the Army service applications, and signed on the line. The recruitment man in military uniform shook their hands and thanked them for their civic courage and patriotism.

The next morning, Adam had a terrible hangover. He was only able to think about how to "get a fix." He totally forgot about the Army application he had completed the day before.

Soon the mailman brought Adam a summons, instructing him to arrive at City Hall on a particular day, where he would be informed of the details of his future military service.

Understandably, his parents were in shock. Adam, the pacifist, was in shock also. But what could be done? The form had been filled out and signed by his hand. If Adam refused to come on the appointed day, he would be under threat of arrest and have been taken anyway, but to the infantry. Otherwise, he could choose the type of troop to join. Adam chose the medical forces, comforting himself with the thought that he would not have to shoot. A month and a half later, Adam was already in a training camp in South Carolina, where he learned the combat attendant basics. Three months later, he was sent to Vietnam. "Enjoy the ride, kid."

Funny story, isn't it?

However, very soon comedy gave way to tragedy. From the very first day, Adam was confronted with the horrors of war. Armed with a handgun, he carried out wounded soldiers from the battlefield, injected them with morphine, and dressed their wounds. In the field hospital, he assisted during surgeries. To survive, he shot at enemies—Vietnamese soldiers—never knowing if he killed any of them. He fell under the shelling and suffered contusion. After that, he was discharged from the Army and returned to the United States.

He drank alcohol in the Army and swallowed narcotic pills in order not to go insane. I'll say! Every day seeing blood, wounds, torn pieces of human hands and legs, corpses. Once Adam returned home, he began to drink and use without control. He was mentally broken and knew no other way to cope with his shattered soul. In those years, the United States did not have the variety of medical centers for war veterans it does today. Back then, little was known about the connections between traumatic experience and drug addiction.

Adam drank and got high for more than ten years. He was admitted to psych wards and detoxes. He visited a therapist. He attended veteran meetings of Anonymous Alcoholics. He went to the synagogue as well in the hope that religion would help. He relapsed, drinking and sniffing again. With great difficulty, finally, he crawled out of this ditch.

Yes, that ride on the carousel in Astroland Amusement Park had come at a very high price.

"Well, that's my destiny. But I do not regret anything," Adam told me while we were walking down the street during lunch, sipping coffee from Starbucks. "During the war, I gained an invaluable experience and began to look at many things differently. Of course, it cost me. I had to fight with depression, PTSD, and alcohol addiction. But I learned how to forgive people, understand their weaknesses and their pains, just like everything I experienced." He looked somewhere into the distance, adjusting the glasses on his nose.

"You see buddy, this is what I understood: alcohol is the best cure for the psychological trauma of war. Alcohol numbs that terrible past, which is always with you. That past does not leave you alone. War never ends in your soul. Years, decades, nights, and days—you have to fight, to take the wounded from the battlefield under fire and explosions. It is best to face this war with a bottle of whiskey. The worst part is withdrawal in the morning, and you have to drink again. Then depression begins . . . I read somewhere that every day in the States about twenty veterans commit suicide. It's hard to comprehend, Pete. Imagine today twenty more of our veterans will kill themselves! Have you ever called the Veteran hospital? No? Do it, and an answering machine will immediately provide you with the extension for the hotline in case you have suicidal thoughts and want to kill yourself. I had called that number too."

Listening to Adam, I couldn't help but recall my years of service in the Russian army, in which I served for 2 years before being admitted to the College (in Russia every young man must serve in the army). Many soldiers in our platoon loved booze. We drank as long as we had money and could get our hands on alcohol. We drank not only vodka and wine but also moonshine. Some even drank cologne. We drank at any opportunity, using any dishware available when we didn't have mugs. Pots, bowls. I remember we even unscrewed the headlight cover from an armored vehicle to use as an impromptu drinking vessel.

At the time I served in the army there was a second war between Russia and Chechnya (Russian North Caucasus region) going on. I did not take part in that war, although it was a good possibility. A few soldiers from our platoon were deployed there. Many soldiers, including me, actually asked to go there, submitting written requests. The propaganda worked. It was poured into our ears every day that the Chechens were our enemies and that the US was helping them to destroy great Russia. In order to protect our Motherland we have to destroy Chechens and in the future, invade Ukraine, Baltic States, and other "unfriendly countries." I asked to be sent to the war, and if they had deployed me there, I would have been glad. I was nineteen years old then, just as brainwashed by propaganda and turned into a robot as most of my Army comrades. I was a young man, and I wanted to be a hero.

Who knows what kind of war hero I would have been if I was thrown into the trenches and saw real blood and death? Would I have brought a lot of grief and suffering to other people? Would I then need to be treated for PTSD and drug addiction like Adam?

Fortunately, it didn't happen. My fate spared me.

In our clinic, Adam was a primary counselor for veteran patients from the Korean, Vietnam, Iraq, or Afghan wars. I remember awful cries and cursing from the patients in his office: "Fuck all! I'll shoot this bitch! . . . I'll buy an M-16 and shoot all these scumbag bureaucrats in the Veterans' Department!"

How many times did Liza and I and other counselors approach Adam's office, thinking it was time to save Adam and call the police. We opened the door: an enraged patient stood in the "gun for preparation" pose, yelling, "I'll kill! I'll shoot!" We gestured to Adam asking whether we should call 911. He responded in a calm but determined sign: do not call anywhere, the situation is under control. After a while, that patient, indeed, calmed down.

"How do you manage them?" I asked Adam, impressed by his clinical skills. "What is your secret?"

"No secret. At all times, I try to remember what this person has gone through."

In fact, he gave every patient time to the max. He often spent more time with them than the usual 45 minutes of an individual session. His "unprofessional" approach in spending a significant amount of time with each patient might have really annoyed Francesca. However, I never saw Francesca make any negative remarks to Adam, and it was evident that she appreciated him a great deal. Francesca used to visit him in his office and for some reason often stayed there a long time. Adam would close the little window in the door with a cardboard sign saying "Session in progress. Don't disturb!" as if there really was a psychotherapy session.

Soon I found out that Francesca's youngest son, against the will of the parents, joined the U.S. military as an ordinary Marine.

One day, Francesca came out of Adam's office with red and teary eyes. Her son was being sent to Afghanistan . . .

"NOT EVEN A DOLLAR"

The manager of the sober house was a man of about forty years old by the name of Jim. He was a former patient and resident of a sober house. Jim had recently completed treatment and started his professional career in this field.

This was an angry, defiant man who, after long years of humiliation, was given power over his own kind, those just like him only yesterday. From rags to riches. Jim was disgustingly ingratiating toward the clinic personnel, whereas he was cruel and rough with the patients, humiliating them. He reminded them every time that they are nothing and no one. He'd yell at them and hurry them out quickly into the van as if herding cattle. He acted like a tough boss over the patients, appointing as his assistants (called sergeants or captains) those he liked and who were power-hungry. Jim was in charge of expelling from the sober house those who were caught using drugs or violating the rules. Such expulsions he executed harshly and with great pleasure.

Francesca appeared to keep her distance from her faithful servant Jim because he was horrendous, and she did not want to be associated with him. However, I suspect his work was so satisfactory that she privately valued his dedication and readiness to serve.

The patients hated Jim. They often complained about Jim's arbitrariness and the horrific living conditions in the sober houses. Without enough beds, they slept on mattresses or box springs on the floor. The heating and air conditioning didn't work. Countless cockroaches and other insects lived in the sober houses. Mice, too.

I no longer trusted my ears. But the patients would sometimes lift their sweaters and t-shirts to show bloody bites from bedbugs. I believed my eyes.

Theft flourished there. Residents stole money, music players, and cell phones from each other. Everyone suffered from a lack of privacy and lack of personal space. Not all of them practiced good hygiene. Some took strong psychotropic drugs prescribed by doctors, and these medications caused a particularly unpleasant odor. All this was in addition to Jim the power abuser and his sergeants and captains overseeing the facilities. This was one hell of a treatment.

The patients called me "dude." Indeed, for them, I was a Russian dude who didn't understand a damn thing about drug addiction, prison, or life on the streets. "Bookworm, try to teach us something." Still, recognizing my sympathy toward their needs, patients tried to go easier on me.

As the defender of miserable folks, I went to our director Francesca, who had returned from another boutique with a pile of fashionable clothes. I told her that the conditions in the sober house were very bad. Something needed to be done.

Franchi blinked her charming eyes. She had clearly just come from a store filled with silks, leathers, furs, music, fitting rooms, and mirrors. Now she had to hear about broken air conditioners, cockroaches, mice . . . Pee-ew.

She interrupted me impatiently, replying that she knew all about it and measures had already been taken. She reminded me I am not a house superintendent but a substance abuse counselor, and I should concern myself with psychotherapy. She casually noted that maintenance and repair services today are expensive, and all our staff in the clinic want to get paid. Our conversation ended.

After I left Francesca, I poured out my frustration to Liza. But she didn't always take my side:

"Yes, you're right. I know, Franchi is stingy about money. But listen, kid, don't you think patients might be leading you on? They bullshit about other things so they don't have to talk about drug use. Addicts don't want to talk about drugs. They will tell you about anything else in the world, including bed bugs and mice. They'll turn their hearts inside out. But they avoid talking about drugs. It's shameful and it's scary to open up. So they complain about their living conditions. *Capisce?*"

I had no doubt that I'd made a mistake choosing this profession. I didn't know who to blame for this. I was applying my real-life experience of my father drinking, but somehow that didn't help me. I didn't understand these people at all. I didn't see how anything I was doing was helping. More and more often, confusion and despair seized me.

Should I leave? Give up? Choose some other career? Or maybe go back to Russia altogether? Everything familiar to me is there. At night I reminisced about the apple orchard near my five-story building. The branches of the apple trees came up almost to the windows of my apartment on the second floor. I slept on the balcony in the summer, on a squeaky cot. I inhaled the aroma of apples. I listened to the birds sing in the morning as I lay bundled up in my woolen blanket. Oh, how good it was, how good . . . But there is Putin's regime, there is no freedom, and a new Russian invasion of another country is on its way.

Now here came an American morning of a new workday. My thoughts washed away with the morning shower, right down the drain. I dressed quickly and hurried to the bus stop.

I didn't understand at the time that I had come across the "powerhouses"—the most difficult patients, the drug users of the criminal world who were homeless. Tough guys. Tougher do not exist. How was I supposed to know that in brilliant, magnificent

New York, in addition to the polished and energetic stock traders on Wall Street and the happy tourists in Times Square, there is an entire army of unlucky characters who have hit rock bottom? And we are not talking about numbers in the single digits but in the tens of thousands. Maybe even hundreds of thousands.

The System sends this army through three streams: to prison, to drug and mental health treatment institutions, and to halfway houses. If someone slips away from the System, finds himself on the street, using and stealing and robbing again, this generally does not last long. The fallen will quickly be picked up and funneled back into one of these streams. These people have almost completely lost their skills for community life. Very few are able to pull through.

To this day, I wonder why I didn't slam the door shut and leave the substance abuse field forever. What forces kept me there?

It's not clear how long I was wracked by doubt and where this would lead. But the situation resolved itself in unexpected ways. It all began . . . with a common toothache. My molar became a serious blight on my life. It had ached from time to time for a long while, but then the pain became unbearable. The dentist took x-rays and delivered his verdict: He needed to do a root canal and put in a crown. Yet the x-ray also discovered that the maxillary bone had started to decay. I would need surgery.

However, the medical aspect of the problem frightened me far less than the financial one. As soon as the dentist announced the price, my tooth stopped aching immediately. But, alas, not for long.

We were provided with medical insurance at work, but it wasn't very good, nor did it cover non-routine dental procedures. Now, I sat in my tiny half-basement apartment, on the edge of the Capital of the World. I sat with my puffy left cheek, swallowing aspirin and sulkily calculating how much time it would take to save enough money to pay for the root canal, crown, and surgery. I even considered going back to Time Warner as a security guard, part-time during the evening shift, to guard my damn trashcan. "Oh Lord, won't you buy me a Mercedes Benz?"

What was good about Francesca was her unusual sense of fairness. None of our colleagues would be given an exception—all were exploited equally. She extracted as much as she could from everyone and paid us the minimum she could get away with. The staff grumbled and threatened to go elsewhere for better pay. But of the ten counselors who worked there, Bob was the only one who actually left.[5]

Oh, how dreadful it is to go to your bosses for such an awful matter! Don't bother them!

Don't spoil their life! You know how their faces will sink and what kind of deathly gloom will appear in their eyes when you ask them for a raise. Who on Earth is less happy than they are at that moment?

I politely reminded Francesca about the conditions of my employment. When we signed the employment contract, we agreed to an annual review and subsequent raise. Since then, as I reminded her, almost two years had passed and it was time to discuss this very delicate issue.

Franchi stared at me, wobbling her head which sported a freshly styled haircut. Her eyes were clouded by sincere sadness:

"Pete, my dear, you know that I love you . . . "

I looked at her in surprise. Had I heard correctly? "Pete, my dear . . . I love you . . . "

"But now," she continued, "the clinic is undergoing some difficult times. You can't imagine how hard it is to run this business; competition is crazy. Forgive me, but I can't do it. I can't raise your salary even a dollar."

So that's how it is? Today, right now, I'll buy myself a new suit and tie. I'll update my resume. I'll lie at the interview, say I'm an expert with vast experience and I know exactly how to treat this damn drug addiction!

In America, we have a wonderful tradition of giving a person who leaves a good luck card. "Pete, good luck with your new job! Don't forget us! Call us! I believe in you!" There was cake, pizza, and Pepsi. I remember Francesca's emotional farewell speech, Adam's brotherly hug, and Liza's watery eyes.

I still have and cherish to this day that card with its good luck wishes.

PART THREE

I started a new job at a hospital-based outpatient clinic in the Bronx. I hit the jackpot. My current salary was almost double the last, and they offered excellent health insurance. The clinic, however, was not in the main hospital buildings, but in a different, poor, and high-crime Bronx neighborhood.

Russian-speaking immigrants had lately come to increasingly populate this area, which in turn affected the patient demographic in the substance abuse clinic. Drug counselor who could work with both Russian-speaking and American patients was in need.

Now I had my own office and didn't have such a crazy workload. The sense of an endless flow of patients, like log piles traveling downstream, had disappeared. I now had the opportunity to listen more attentively to what they were saying.

Unfortunately, I soon learned this place had a different problem—politics. Endless gossip, snitching, whispering, betrayal, fighting for positions, for favors from bosses. Workers were always forming alliances and battling each other. One group would oppose the administration and the other would stay loyal to it. This was the working climate. Anyone who didn't want to take part in this cut-throat competition would shut the door of his office and hang a sign in the door: "Session in progress! Please, do not disturb!"

A FEMININE FACE

CHARMING CYNTHIA

Up until then, I had only dealt with the tough guys who didn't come by choice but were mandated for treatment by courts and prosecutors. And suddenly—here was a lady. She was my first female patient.

To describe Cynthia as beautiful would be an understatement. She was Puerto Rican, fit, and very charming. She usually came to the clinic in a stylish, form-fitting denim suit, drawing the eye to her body. It's a pity that such a naturally attractive girl disfigured herself with obvious massive silicone implants. Cynthia danced in a strip club.

She needed a letter from me for the court, where the judge was to decide if she could see her child and how often. Her five-year-old son was living with her husband, who had filed for divorce and sole custody of their son.

I will admit that, back then, I spent some lonely evenings occasionally cheering up my bachelorhood a bit by visiting strip clubs. There, amid the tenderness of women who led you slowly through the darkness of the club, it was easy to forget everything and to believe, even if for a moment, that the world was full of gentleness and warmth. My acquaintance with Cynthia happened just as I decided to give up the habit of frequenting strip clubs, where enchanting ladies would skillfully devastate my wallet. It's true that everything happens for a reason. Meeting Cynthia turned into a challenge for me.

She often went on trips with her boyfriends to relax, snort coke, and drink. It's true she hadn't hit rock bottom yet. What bottom? What are you talking about? Cynthia gave the impression of being a carefree, almost happy young woman, living the life, even though she hadn't been to college and hadn't even finished high school. She thought of herself as a bit clueless and a scatterbrain. Her husband, she said, was a real bore who cared only about annoying domestic routines. But Cynthia wanted fire, light, music, crazy love . . .

What could be done? She'd fallen in love with yet another playboy and gone on a sweet tour with him, living it up in restaurants and partying in hotels. But soon this gentleman was looking at her as—forgive me—a common whore. And he sent her packing.

Cynthia was very sensitive. Her separations and heartbreaks with men pained her greatly. The Emergency Room of our hospital once called me to confirm some information about Cynthia. It turned out that after yet another admirer left her, she drank, smoked weed, and climbed to the top of a 22-story building to dance on the edge of the roof.

She needed just one document from me for court. She asked me to write that she was "good and clean." She hoped the judge would let her see her son without restrictions. But her husband insisted that she was an active addict and shouldn't be allowed near the child.

What a show she conducted in my office during the sessions! But a chair is not a stage in a strip club. So, she had to find a way to entertain without rising from the chair: She bent her body in different ways, leaned over, pressed her elbows against her chest, and constantly adjusted the straps of her bra.

Looking at Cynthia, I felt transported back to a roaring strip club, to a room of magic smiles and silky-skinned feminine hips. In short, I was fighting my own madness, too.

Once in my office, Cynthia cried seriously and bitterly of how badly everything in her life had turned out, that she was a terrible mother. She said her son, Carlos, was dearer to her than life itself and she couldn't imagine not being able to see him.

"But you still snort coke. And drink booze," I said, fighting to move my eyes from the bulging bosom under her t-shirt. "Think of how badly this may affect your son."

"I won't lie, I do blow occasionally," she admitted. "Sometimes I just want coke so badly, so badly . . . you know what I mean. You also used to get high, right?"

"Yes, a while ago," I answered with a thoughtful air, secretly glad that she considered me "one of them." I had learned that I could pretend to be someone who used to get high. I am one of you! Don't be ashamed. You can be open and honest with me!

"Don't bullshit me! I'm sure you don't even know what a bag of coke looks like! How can you teach me anything? You never used, and on top of it, you're lying!"

When they say that the tips of one's ears burn from shame, it's true. Of all the known expressions of shame, the most painful are those burning ears tips. To know if someone is feeling ashamed, look at their ears, not their eyes!

Having made me feel ashamed, Cynthia again started "dancing" in the chair.

"Fine. If you want the paper for the court, then give me now your urine for toxicology," I said firmly.

She looked at me somewhat tensely.

"I can't. You know, I have . . . my period. When I have my period, I have a lot of pain right here below my tummy, and I get very nervous and cranky. Forgive me, Pete, if I offended you in some way. You're a very nice man, a real amigo. Help me. Write a good letter for me."

I finally gave up and wrote her a letter for the court. Everything I wrote was a lie. Cynthia was already unhappy and thought herself useless and worthless. If they took away her maternal rights, what would she have left? That was my reasoning.

Cynthia was too carefree. And she saw her progressing drug addiction as another type of harmless entertainment.

I may have too. I was still very green. I watched Cynthia with contentment as she walked happily down the corridor of the clinic with her "good letter" in hand. To be honest, I also found myself glancing at the hips she swayed so seductively.

Neither she nor I had any idea what lay ahead.

A few weeks later, she called me and gleefully reported that, thanks to my letter, the judge ruled in her favor. They would allow her to see her son with hardly any restrictions! Now she could completely change her life. She had a whole set of positive plans and goals: to get her GED, to give up stripping and find a more dignified job—like working as a saleswoman at a store, to go to cosmetology school, and then to win back her son, Carlos, so he could live with her.

I wished her good luck.

The last time I heard about Cynthia was a few years later. There was a detox unit in our hospital where the drug users/alcoholics wound up when they were in alcohol withdrawals or dope-sick. The outpatient clinic and detox were connected by a common electronic system; each clinician had access to the data in both divisions.

I once saw Cynthia's first and last name on the list of newly admitted patients to detox. I called there to make sure it was really Cynthia and not someone else with the same name.

There are no miracles. It was that same Cynthia. I spoke on the phone with the counselor from detox and asked about her. I said she was my former patient. I even mentioned her unforgettable charm.

"I'll try to stop by detox tomorrow to see her," I said.

"Why do you want to see her?" my colleague asked coldly. "She's lying in bed; she's scrawny and covered in acne. Nothing charming about her. Just a common, used-up whore."

Could it be said that Cynthia and the hundreds—the thousands—of women like her are very bad and careless mothers? That they love the little bags of drugs more than they love their own children? That because of these mothers, children wind up in the System, looked after by Child Protective Services? That because of these mothers, children are given up to foster care and adoptive homes?

I know, I know, this is all true. And we can't forgive them; we can't feel sorry for them. Let them destroy their own lives—that is their right. But why destroy the lives of their children?

Still, I recall other patients who were like Cynthia. An Italian named Nicole. And Black Sharon. And Jamaican Amelia. They all went to court where they promised, vowed, and sobbed, begging the judges to not take away their parental rights. Sometimes they were allowed to take the children home at specified times. Their faces would shine with such joy then! Sometimes they brought their children to the clinic to show them off and brag about them.

These women all painted their future with the same rosy hue: they would finish treatment, give up prostitution forever, and the courts would fully reinstate their parental rights. They would take up a real profession and bring their children home. They would buy the best clothes and electronics for them. They would, they would...

They dreamed the way many drug users dream, painting pictures exclusively with rosy tones because grays were the dominant shades of their present.

Sadly, not all of them passed through the gates of that imagined paradise. After yet another relapse, several plunged with despair into even greater depravity and drug addiction than before. I know one woman who, after her maternal rights were removed permanently by the court, attempted suicide by letting oven gas seep into her apartment. Thankfully, a neighbor smelled gas and called 911 before it was too late. An ambulance and a fire truck arrived. The woman ended up in the psych ward.

Some male colleagues advised me: If possible, it is better not to have women as patients. It was easier, they said, to work with hardcore criminals than with women, especially young and beautiful ones.

"Buddy, you can't imagine how they behave," one of my colleagues, a man by the name of Edward, shared with me. "Women . . . you will never understand when they lie or speak the truth. I'm not sure they even know themselves. I've had them flirt with me. A few stripped their clothes off in my office. Some asked me out for drinks, offered me pills, and wanted to get high together. I've learned to deal with all that. But the tough thing to handle is these mind games they play, when they reveal their secrets to you and expose one intimate thing after another. And when you think that this is the last layer and this dance is over, it turns out it's just beginning. You are tired of fighting with yourself. You want her and you fuck her in your dreams. Man, what kind of treatment is possible after that?"

In this respect, I was not an exception in this matter. Female patients, especially young and beautiful ones, became a great temptation for me. I knew that intimate relations between a counselor and a patient are considered a violation of professional ethics, and, if proven, may lead to either termination or revoked credentials.

Still, I wanted to be liked by them. I wanted to impress them with my education, mind, and polite manners. Of course, during the sessions, I repeated that our common goal was their treatment and only treatment. Oh, yes . . . The female patients quickly guessed what a "skillful" counselor they were dealing with. They shared jokes, responded to my courtesy, and attended our sessions in clothes that would be perfect for a porn magazine photoshoot. In short, they wanted to be attractive to me. Why not? I could be attracted to them, but they couldn't be attracted to me?

At the same time, I was always aware that I saw them as easy and dirty women. It was a challenge for me to learn how to rid myself of the bad habit of flirting with female patients.

And most importantly: how to not despise them.

In any addiction clinic, one can boldly assert that the fairer sex is much less represented than men. What's the cause of this?

I think it is because a woman by her nature has a greater sense of duty and responsibility to herself and her family than a man does; this helps her steer clear of dangerous adventures.

There is a popular opinion that women are more successful than men in the fight against drug addiction. This is probably true. For all their perceived love for drama and emotionality, women are actually more realistic than men. Thus, they often manage to create a solid inner foundation. When the time comes, earnestness and determination shine through. I have my former female patients who have stayed clean for years, gotten married, became employed, and raised children.

At the same time, a woman's drug addiction is worse than a man's because the female body is more fragile when it comes to drugs and alcohol; it gets damaged more severely and quickly than the male body. Moreover, the emotional consequences are catastrophic for a woman. A man most often obtains money for drugs by stealing or robbing. A woman's most accessible and common route is the flesh trade.

And don't forget that a lot of money is required—a lot! Crack and heroin are really expensive, and there is no holiday discount. Some drug users spend a hundred dollars on drugs—A DAY! Some spend two hundred. One can meet some champions who spend up to three hundred daily! And someone who smokes crack can spend a thousand per day.

Yes, drug users are very creative storytellers; many of them like hyperbole and adding color to their heroism to impress others. And they like to impress themselves as well. Nonetheless, one to two hundred dollars a day for drugs is no exaggeration. Where do they get this kind of money? Holding a job and using drugs daily don't go together. Work interferes. Just try to count how many times a day a woman must sell her body to get high.

I'm not familiar with the exact rates for prostitutes in New York City. Moreover, the business is very diversified: from prestigious escort services costing thousands of dollars, to street prostitution in the poorest areas of New York, where one fuck costs twenty dollars, I've been told.

Any type of prostitution is almost always connected with drug use. First, it is less revolting and more tolerable to engage in an act of prostitution when one is high. Second, clients often want the call girl to drink with them elegantly and sometimes snort, too.

The girls in our clinic were very ashamed of being prostitutes and preferred not to talk about it in front of anyone. However, among themselves, they would argue about which type of prostitution—an escort service, stripping, or street hooking—was less shameful and more profitable.

WALKING ON THE EDGE

Many of the women who came through my door, regardless of race, nationality, or country of origin, were sexually abused, harassed, or molested in their past—in childhood or adolescence. Has this psychological trauma had an effect on their later fate, and on the fact that they've taken up the syringe? Without a doubt. Such trauma is not quickly and easily treated. It isn't just a scratch on the arm.

Frida was a nice girl of twenty from a family of Orthodox Jews. She finished Jewish religious school and went to college, but she soon quit her studies and wound up in our clinic. Her drug addiction wasn't that bad yet, but Frida definitely "had a problem." From time to time, she used cocaine and sold pills. She and her parents clashed, but even worse, she was constantly sparking up affairs with men. Patients fell in love with her. She slept with a few of them. She had piercings, tattoos on her neck, shoulders, and forearms, as she said, exactly the same style Amy Winehouse had. Amy Winehouse was her idol.

I tried to reconnect Frida with her parents and advised her to return to college, get a job, take up yoga—shortly, to do anything healthy and helpful. Frida refused everything. Any conversation with her about God or the possibility to get her back to religion invoked a very angry reaction in her.

I had a gut feeling that Frida went through some sexually traumatic experience, but when asked, she denied it.

There was a good tradition in the clinic of organizing cultural outings for the patients: to bring them to the cinema, to concerts, to dances, so that they would experience fun and pleasure without drugs. At that time, I was assigned to bring the group to the famous Yankee Stadium to watch a baseball game.

Clearly, the patients shouldn't drink beer. It doesn't matter if it's a hard drink or a light one. One drop of alcohol is the same as a hundred. Booze is booze. All the patients who came with me to the stadium were again given strict warnings on this account. Frida was in our group.

Once inside the stadium, she right away made the acquaintance of two forty-year-old men. Within a blink of an eye, the two had their arms around her and she was holding a can of beer. During the game, these two tomcats tried to persuade Frida to leave with them. She likely promised them something, and they were happy to get on so easily with such a pretty girl. If not for my strict warning, there's no doubt Frida would not be on the bus with us after the game but would have headed in another direction.

It became clear to me then that she was walking on the edge without realizing it.

I saw Frida again several months after she had quit the treatment program. I met her in the ER of our hospital. Frida sat on the bed, wrapped in a hospital gown. She was trembling. She recognized me and gave a weak smile. The fresh burns and red marks on her neck and hands confused me. She told me that on the street she had met a Caucasian man who introduced himself as a stockbroker. He seemed intelligent and even courteous. They walked around the city and then went into a bar, drank some beer, and sniffed something in a dark corner. Then they went to his friend's house. Frida woke up early the next morning under the subway overpass. She didn't remember what had happened or how she had gotten there.

Most likely, they had put some narcotic pills—so-called date rape drugs—in her glass of beer and she had lost consciousness. Her clothing was torn. And her whole body was in pain. It's clear that they had sexually assaulted her. But that's not all. The men she was accosted by were sexual perverts, sadists.

Looking at me, Frida suddenly lowered her robe from her shoulder and I was horrified—her tattooed shoulders, chest, and back were covered in small cuts and bloody burns, as if someone put out cigarettes all over her body.

"I knew something was fucking wrong with me since I was thirteen," she said quietly, looking down.

"What do you mean? What's wrong with you?" I asked.

"Why else would he fuck me? It's all my fault he fucked me."

"Who?"

"My neighbor. I was in eighth grade then, and he was about forty. I fully trusted him . . . After he fucked me the first time, he told me I had to return to him the next day or I would be 'in trouble.' I was terrified and I went back the next day, and it happened again. Since that time, I was always afraid that I would be found out. I was afraid, afraid, afraid . . . Shit!" she screamed out and suddenly jumped up from the hospital bed and started pummeling me with her fists.

I covered my face, then managed to get a tight hold on her just as psych technicians ran in. The psych technicians restrained Frida and started to walk her back towards her bed. A doctor shortly appeared and said, "Help her lie down. I'll make an order for an injection."

This is also the face of female addiction.

Just a minute! What about love? Courtship, passion, and sighs? Flowers and chocolates? Yes, these must be described as well. Cupid rushes into substance abuse clinics, and especially so because passions run hotter where men outnumber women.

Love in this case is a bridge where a charming gentleman carries an open-hearted girl across to a dangerous shore. Females usually become drug users thanks to their boyfriends. Men are in the know. Men are the foragers. Men know from whom and how much to buy; they know how to snort or cook and shoot. From the start, they want their girlfriend to experience this sweet, harmless high. Of course, they don't suggest it without a selfish motive—no way. Men have their interests. It's good to be married to a hardworking wife who brings her money back to the nest. A drug user—oh, how he needs money! But a working wife has a serious flaw: She doesn't like that you are covered in needle marks, that you are skinny and jobless. And that you spend long periods of time locked in the bathroom. Such a wife grumbles at first, then cries, and threatens divorce. It sometimes happens that she changes the locks on the door or leaves, bringing her child with her.

In contrast, the drug user's girlfriend is a comrade in arms. She gets it. She isn't going to complain or yell. She's going to assist. With a woman, it's easier to steal clothing from expensive boutiques—security guards check her less often, and her fingers are nimbler at cutting off the electronic tags. Moreover, she is a devoted friend who will give you everything she has, including her bags of drugs. In most cases, female drug users are very true to their men; they don't cheat on them and tolerate and forgive all.

A man who is flat broke, desperate for money, and without any other means to obtain it can sell his junkie girlfriend to someone. This is often the *finita la commedia* of the love story.

In substance abuse clinics, passions are boiling over. Women who have experienced debauchery, arrests, and violence flourish in drug clinics. Men compete for them and chase after them. Although we clinicians call on the patients to be celibate and refrain from intimate relations, romantic liaisons arise ceaselessly. In the soil of jealousy, conflicts thrive, threatening to escalate into battles—as in a tournament between knights from days of old.

Furious wives show up saying that they worked so hard to drag their husbands to the clinic to be treated, and then the bastard took on a mistress there. Husbands wait in their cars not far from the clinic, watching so that their wives don't get too involved, don't forget they have a family, and after the therapy go straight home.

Sometimes this leads both to divorce and wife-beating. Female drug users are often beaten. Their husbands, boyfriends, or simply other junkies beat them.

"PEE-PEE TIME": DRAMA IN THE RESTROOM

I once brought a patient named William to the restroom. We walked to the bathroom together, chatting along the way. I gave him the plastic cup.

My hand freezes above this white sheet of paper. I question if it is necessary to talk about this. The theme isn't exactly literary. What should I do? The poets and writers in the XIX century had it easy when the subjects of their poems and novels were forests, orchards, and flocks of cranes above the lovely meadows. Roses, nightingales. Poetry sang out, touching the hearts of readers and making them cry tears of delight for the beauty of life. Where are you, cranes and nightingales? Where did you fly? Have you abandoned us forever? Has life changed so dramatically that a reader can no longer enjoy literary tales of nightingales or smell the scent of roses, and instead—at the decree of the author—must enter (forgive me) a common bathroom and read about how someone will pee. *O tempora, o mores*! Oh, times, Oh, customs!

Of course, this is definitely not a theme for a literary work. Art should concern itself with the soul of man and nothing else. However, this work isn't fiction and the subject of our interest is specific. Our character is a person with a drug problem, and we are trying to discern the incomprehensible and frightening phenomenon of drug addiction. A toxicology test or, simply put, a urine screening, was, is, and will always be one of the important parts of treating a drug user. "Pee-pee time." That's what patients jokingly call the test.

I could even say that the treatment of drug and alcohol dependence takes place not only in a counselor's office, at AA/NA (Alcoholics Anonymous/Narcotics Anonymous) meetings, or in a church or synagogue if the addict is a religious person. The toilet is no less important a location, where the truth is often revealed, where the future will be determined, where the mask falls from one's face, and where all kept in darkness will come to light. We can even say that "clean" or "dirty" urine is the indicator of how successful the treatment is.

No way! This is all deeper and more complex, and we shouldn't relegate the inner conflicts of a man to such a point of view. His internal spiritual struggles, his ups and downs, should not be evaluated so primitively with the formulaic phrase: "Is his urine clean or dirty?" But, alas, the reality is such that it often all comes down to this. What is the value of words? We know that many active drug addicts are master bullshit artists—they take oaths and offer convoluted speeches. They have violated these sworn oaths so many times as to make what they say worthless. Hence, we believe only in the "pee-pee" test. The test doesn't lie.

There are many different kinds of toxicology test kits: white plastic sticks, special cups with panel markings, paper strips to place on a tongue. The test results are determined in those special laboratories that receive the plastic cups from many different clinics on a daily basis. Each drug remains in the urine for a specified period of time. For example: alcohol—less than a day; cocaine—three or four days; marijuana—about a month. Users know this already. There's nothing overly scientific about it.

But there is a science—or an art rather—to the user's ability to give the counselor someone else's clean urine if his is dirty. Here we are entering the realm of the magical. However, all in due course.

So, I went with William to the restroom. I gave him the usual plastic cup to pee into, and I stood behind him. He walked up to the urinal and unzipped his jeans. "Oh, the pin! I bet there was a con artist in here, right before me," he joked. William wasn't a newbie to substance abuse clinics, so the ordinary metal pin lying in the urinal told him a lot.

At first, I was bewildered by the presence of used condoms in the men's room at the clinics. Yes, condoms are often found on the floor, in the urinals, and in the trashcans. No matter how much I tried to use my imagination, I could not understand where the used condoms had come from and why they were there. It would be absurd to assume that a booming sex life was flourishing in the bathrooms of substance abuse clinics.

It was all very simple: "dirty" patients bring someone else's "clean" urine in a condom. So, this is a reliable, proven method. They attach the condom to the belt of their jeans and let it hang in their underwear. Then, cup in hand, with their back to the counselor, they quietly remove the pin from their pocket, unbutton their pants, and pierce a hole in the condom. Psss. Then they dispose of all this unneeded "equipment." That is why pins and condoms abound in the bathrooms of drug clinics. There is nothing romantic or sexual about it.

Rarely will a patient admit that he is "dirty." More often he will say that he is "clean" when he is not. Yet, such emotions blaze in the restroom. Such drama occurs when it turns out that their "clean" is not clean, but dirty. The loud speech that ensues! The lies flow like a river. The patient alleges that the stick is bad and states that the counselor doesn't trust anybody and stands like a dragon behind his back looking over his shoulder. How many times have I had to listen to accusations made by angry patients who have tried to submit fake urine to me, tell me that I am a racist, a sex pervert, and worse than a police officer (as well as many other identities I never knew about myself.)

The patient—this sphinx with pensive, honest-looking eyes—poses a complicated riddle to the counselor. Every time, the counselor awaits the answer, not only from the patient but also from the plastic test stick. Will the narrow red stripe appear on the plastic stick? Until the stick is in the cup and the chemical reaction is processed, the individual is subject to doubt.

Just think for a moment: Nobody believes a man until they dip the plastic stick into the cup he just peed in. How humiliating!

UNDERGROUND CITY

So much water has passed under the bridge since I entered the substance abuse field! I came in as a casual passerby, never imagining the journey on which I was embarking. Could I have known at the time that I was choosing much more than just a profession?

I was dating a woman named Victoria who had recently graduated from college and worked as an office manager. I moved to the Bronx, near Riverdale, and rented a nice one-bedroom apartment.

The more I learned about the Big Apple, the more I fell in love with it. I loved its damp, fog enveloping the tops of the skyscrapers, the 100-degree summer heat, the falling leaves in autumn, the four-lined avenues, the ocean bays, the wind, the sleet. New York, New York!

But I discovered another city within the "capital of the world" whose existence I had not suspected. It is an underground city not marked on any map, although it is densely populated. I noticed here and there the active drug users: the skinny young men standing on street corners, shifting impatiently from one foot to the other. I saw them on buses and in the subway when they tried to pickpocket someone or steal a woman's purse. Some worked in stores, taxicabs, and restaurants.

Every morning, the superintendent of our building would sweep the sidewalk near the entrance. He was surprised when I told him that the little empty plastic bags he was throwing into the trash used to be filled with cocaine. (A few tenants in the building were dipping and dabbing in coke.)

I would see patients of mine—past, present, and future ones—in bars, barbershops, and auto repair shops. Of course, I would also see them next to the liquor stores. Vicky and I went into an expensive boutique on Park Avenue and I suddenly recognized my patient—she was trying to remove electronic tags discreetly from some expensive shirts. At a bar not far from Wall Street, a man wearing the business suit of a stockbroker came out of the restroom; he was twitching after snorting a line of coke. The shattered right window of someone's car told me that a drug user had broken the glass at night and stolen the GPS from the glove compartment to sell for a few bags. One clerk at the post office who was fumbling with a package for nearly half an hour was nodding out on methadone.

I don't wish to say that New York is a city of drug users. Most likely, there are no more of them in the "capital of the world" than in any other major urban area. But now I clearly distinguish this world.

Once, when Victoria and I were on our way to my place, I was stupid enough to share my observations with her. She said, "If you want me to come live with you, find an apartment in a better area." However, she softened her tone after we walked about the area she was living in and I pointed out what she had never paid attention to before. Although the neighborhood was considered good, even there "my friends" (as she called them) abounded.

CRAPPY PORTFOLIO

Perhaps there is no jollier group of people than drug users! No matter how low fate has dragged them down, or how high it has raised them, they find a reason to laugh. Their genre is not tragedy, but tragicomedy. In no other place—theater, cinema, or even the circus—will you encounter such roaring laughter as you find in drug treatment clinics!

This is all so strange because there is hardly any other place where you will find such an abundance of sorrow and grief in all different forms. Close your eyes and point to any drug user, and without fail you will hear a story of abuse, arrests, and suicide attempts. Despite this, substance abuse clinics rumble with laughter. It is hard to say if this is due to the addicts' levity and lack of seriousness or their resilience and survival skills.

In this bizarre world, however, there is a category of people who do not laugh. They rarely make jokes. Humor and laughter do not belong in their scope of existence, although they may have once been cheerful people with a good sense of humor. But their lives changed. Changed so that all that was bright and cheerful was no more. These people rarely smile . . . only in that singular moment when their son or daughter marks a month, six months, or a year of being clean! What a moment of joy! "Clean!" The lips of a mother or father form a smile. A real smile.

The first in many years. But how anxious is the soul? "And if he relapses? Where is he right now? God forbid he ran back to his dealer...."[6]

Sean, a 70-year-old Irish American, comes to mind. He tried to save his 32-year-old son, Frank.

Frank appeared in the clinic for the first time under pressure from his father. Sean noticed that something "wasn't right" with his son. Indeed, Frank abused Xanax, buying pills from a neighbor. He and his girlfriend had split up and his job was in jeopardy.

I advised Frank that he was playing with fire and that the pills would only create new problems. However, Frank didn't listen to me and argued that the "Xanax helps me relax a little."

Father and son disappeared after a few sessions and then turned up again two years later. By then, Frank had stopped experimenting with pills and moved on to shooting heroin. He looked like a madman. His eyes rolled around and there were scary-looking abscesses on his arms. He couldn't sit still even for a minute. He pressed his briefcase to his chest, not wanting to part with it. It was easy to guess that the briefcase was full of dope bags and syringes.

Frank asked for help. He was tired of living that way. He'd gone so low as to steal fire extinguishers and sell them on the black market. Once upon a time, he'd worked as a computer programmer at a prestigious company.

I told him that, first of all, he needed to go to detox and sober up for a week. He reluctantly agreed. While I looked for a detox for him, Frank, who was sitting next to me, took a needle from his pocket and poked at the rotten abscesses on his arm. By doing this, he was clearly in bliss—dope users love the needle. Just touching the needle to their body, especially the place they shoot up, brings them incredible pleasure. When I found a detox and told Frank, he clutched his briefcase to his chest and ran to the bathroom. He locked himself inside a stall and shot up. He would have to go to detox and leave dope! How would he manage to survive?

Meanwhile, his old father Sean was sitting in the waiting room. For sure, he blamed himself for divorcing his wife, an alcoholic, and for raising his son alone. He should have shown his son more warmth and care. That's why Frank was having so much trouble.

When he found out that the detox would accept Frank, Sean was hopeful, got his son in the car, and drove him to the hospital.

Frank left detox that day or the next. Drug treatment is voluntary. Until it becomes mandatory.

I can still see old Sean, a short, puffy-cheeked man who often wore a Yankees baseball cap. He used the word "portfolio" to describe Frank's briefcase.

Sean was a straightforward man who didn't put up with any dubiousness or over-complication. He had no idea what kind of treacherous serpent he was dealing with now. Every time father and son showed up in my office and the three of us together would try to brainstorm solutions, Sean would say:

"Frankie, let's forget everything from the past. I won't remind you of how much money you stole from me. I know, son, that you're a great guy. You were a smart, good, first-class computer programmer. Throw that crappy portfolio in the trash and be done with it. Okay?"

Frank would nod in agreement. But he also pressed the portfolio even more tightly to his chest.

Sean left no stone unturned, looking for help: lawyers, the city health services, and the Treatment Court. Every time, hopeful, he'd show me a new piece of paper with the name and address of another agency which he would go to tomorrow. But everyone told him, "Wait until your Frankie either decides to stop using on his own or until he is arrested for stealing or drug possession. Then he'll be mandated to treatment."

"Why is that?" asked Sean, confused. "My son has lost his mind and could die from an overdose. Everyone sees that, but no one can do anything? I have to wait until he is arrested? I don't understand."

I mentioned to Sean that there is also an option to kick his son out of the house. But Sean was not ready for this "tough love" approach.[7]

"Do you know, Peter, what is the hardest part for me?" he asked me once. "The hardest part is living under constant pressure waiting for THAT phone call".

"Do you mean for a call from the police? At any moment you have to be ready to be informed that your son was arrested, yes?" I suggested.

"Police? If only! I am prepared to hear far worse news."

At one of our city beaches, an annual sandcastle-building completion took place. Vicky and I decided to spend the weekend there.

It was a clear, cool day in August. We stood next to the other spectators and watched as the architects erected sand forts, temples, and palaces. They worked with special blades, brushes, and sharpened sticks, removing the extra grains from columns and bridges. The beach grew into a real city, like Rome or Paris! Cell phone cameras clicked and video cameras filmed the architects. Even journalists were present.

Vicky and I did not wait until the end of the contest and left the sand architects to go swimming. We picked a spot on the beach. Victoria pulled a striped beach towel from the bag and laid it on the sand. She took off her dress to reveal a black bikini. "Because of these corporate parties for the last month, I gained almost an extra pound. Disaster! Tomorrow I will go on a strict diet." She pulled up her black hair into a bun on her head and went swimming.

Rolling up my jeans, I walked along the water.

Night was falling. Beachgoers were starting to leave. Those sand palaces and castles of that enchanted city remained in my mind's eye. Still, why wouldn't God make the world pure and beautiful, and let it remain so? That's what I was thinking. This way, beauty wouldn't disappear and collapse the next day, like the sandy city, but exist forever.

I stood by the jetty and, while contemplating, I looked at a man lying in the sand not far from me. He wore jeans and a red shirt. He was on his back with his arms and legs outstretched. There was something familiar about him. I walked up to him.

Unbelievable! It couldn't be!

"Frank?! Where have ya been? How is your dad doing?" Bending down, I shook his shoulder. "Frankie! Bro!"

No reaction. His face was unusually pale. His mouth was slightly open and his eyes were closed. I started to shake his shoulder more vigorously, then slapped his cheeks.

"Hey, Frank, wake up!"

His head moved in the same direction as my slaps but he showed no signs of life. Next to his sneakers in the sand, I saw a couple of empty bags. Then I realized . . .

I ran to our beach towel where in Vicky's bag, between her makeup kit and a magazine, was my counselor's Narcan kit containing two syringes.

"What's going on?" asked Vicky. She had just emerged from the water. She leaned her head to one side, wringing water out of her wet hair.

"Overdose! Call 911. Quickly!" I ran back to Frank.

I knelt next to him, began to assemble a professional plastic syringe, and put the medicine capsule inside. I was trained many times in the workshops on how to spray medicine intranasal by using this syringe in case of an overdose. But that was only training. Now I had to do it in real life for the first time. Could I do it? Would I remember every step? I was nervous, but at the same time, I was overcome with an indescribable sense of fulfillment and exhilaration because I knew I was doing something at this moment that rendered all of my past deeds insignificant.

I put the tip of the syringe into Frank's nostril and slowly pressed the piston.

"You'll be good now, buddy," I whispered. I had no doubt that Frank would wake up.

Indeed, for a moment it seemed for me that the corners of his grayish lips twitched.

"You see, you see!"

I carefully examined him. A few minutes passed, but his face remained still.

"What is going on? What is going on?" I repeated with bewilderment, tossing one empty syringe and getting another from my Narcan kit. I injected the medicine into his nostril again.

"Wake up, brother, wake up!"

I started to shake him by his shoulders. Then I tried to lift him. His body was cold and heavy. His head went all the way back, and his mouth stayed open.

Angrily I looked at the heavens and said:

"God, for his father's sake, save him!"

A crowd of onlookers gathered around us.

I don't know how much time passed until, finally, the police and ambulance sirens filled the air. Two paramedics carrying a stretcher and two policemen came up to us.

"What happened?" they asked me.

"Overdose," I replied.

One of the paramedics squatted next to Frank, gave him an oxygen mask, and turned on a mobile air compressor.

"Do you know him? Who are you? Do you have ID? Did you inject him?" the policeman interrogated. He looked at me suspiciously, like I was a criminal. Or a drug addict.

"I gave him two capsules of Naltrexone. But it had no effect. I am a substance abuse counselor. I work in a hospital in the Bronx, and he is my former patient."

Meanwhile, one of the paramedics put a rubber pillow under Frank's head. The other paramedic injected his arm and tried to find the pulse on Frank's wrist. They gave him CPR. The cop put on rubber gloves and pulled the wallet and cell phone out of Frank's pockets.

I still couldn't believe this was reality. Certain events disrupt the everyday course of our lives in such a way that our consciousness just cannot keep up; we need time to adapt and get used to them.

"Fuck, we can't do anything. It's too late," the paramedic said and sighed deeply.

At night, Vicky and I were lying in bed together. Vicky fell asleep, but she slept anxiously, tossing and turning all the time from side to side and even talking during sleep like she saw a nightmare. She couldn't get quiet after what she had witnessed today on the beach.

I was thinking about how Sean got THAT phone call a few hours ago and then went to the morgue of the hospital where Frank's corpse was brought in by EMS. How did he manage to do it? Should I go to the funeral? How would I look into his eyes?

Frankie, Frankie. Why didn't you throw that crappy portfolio in the trash and be done with it? Aaah!

WORKING IN ED

"YELLOW GOWNS"

Time passed. The opiate epidemic in the country continued; the number of opiates overdose deaths kept rising. Alarm bells were going off. Various public and private foundations began to allocate resources to fight this new plague.

Two times a week I was assigned to work on the main campus of the hospital, in the Emergency Department. Inside the ED, a special section was dedicated to patients admitted for drug and alcohol abuse or psychiatric conditions. Some of these patients came into the ED on their own while others were brought in by ambulance, called by relatives or attending physicians, and yet others were brought in by the police. Some had their hands cuffed and their feet shackled; these were laid in bed, their arms handcuffed to the metal bedpost, and policemen sat by them. The dangerous ones were guarded by several policemen.

Some of the patients, who came by EMC, were so drunk that they could not stand; such patients were picked up off the street in response to strangers' 911 calls. They had crushed skulls, bloody faces, broken arms and legs. The agitated drunk and psychotic ones were sedated and also tied to the beds with belts. Overdosed drug users were brought in. Suicidal patients were brought in. Homeless people came in drunk, unwashed, in dirty clothes, unshaven and unkempt, the majority giving off a strong odor. Custodians came to this ED section more often than to other parts of the department with water tanks and cleaning supplies. Some young women who injected heroin or took opiate pills came in at all stages of pregnancy. Some of them first learned that they were pregnant in the ED, after a pregnancy test. Some of the patients brought drugs, syringes, and vodka with them into the ED in their bags. They drank and snorted right in their beds—or in the bathroom, so no one would notice.

The majority of patients in this section of the ED were dressed in yellow hospital gowns. Patients had no idea that for the ED employees a yellow gown signaled high alert. Police and special watchmen always had a presence in this area and any relocation of a "yellow gown" always caught their attention.

We called these ED patients "yellow gowns." (Patients in other departments of the ED wore either blue or red gowns; they were not a danger to themselves or others).

Herman, a large black guard, stood by the high pillar in the center of this department, performing the role of "overseer," monitoring and maintaining order. Looking at Herman, I was always amazed that nature could have created such a giant. If any of the patients was ever on the verge of losing control, Herman approached them, and in a steady voice, advised them to calm down and lie back down in bed. If the patient still retained a spark of sanity, looking at Herman, blocking the light of every lamp with his large frame, the patient would return to bed, albeit with resentment. For those in whom the spark of sanity was dimming, and for whom the sight of Herman the giant no longer had the desired effect, the hospital police were called.

Hospital cops, by the way, carried handcuffs but not guns. The city cops bringing the arrested into the ED in shackles and handcuffs were armed, but their guns were not loaded. By the entrance to the ED, there was a tiny room where the cops unloaded their guns. It's understandable: if one of the "yellow gowns" got a hold of a loaded gun, the outcome would be unimaginable.

From this zone patients departed in different directions: some into the psych ED, others were reclaimed by the police, yet others were transferred into the detox or other departments of the hospital. My role was that of a so-called coordinator: with the doctors, I decided where and in what direction to send a "yellow gown."

Not surprisingly, the "yellow gowns area" was rarely empty. Whether day or night, in summer heat or winter cold, there was always a "yellow gown" in the ED, and at any moment a volatile situation could erupt.

Actually, there were fewer "yellow gowns" admitted at the beginning of each month, when they were busy collecting welfare, SSI, SSD, veteran's pension, and other government benefits. In these first few days of each month, the work in the ED passed by relatively calmly. However, in five days' time, once all the money from their benefits had been blown on alcohol and drugs, and withdrawal symptoms were kicking in, the "yellow gowns" burst into the ED like a roaring stream. And on major holidays—New Year's, Christmas, the 4th of July—"yellow gowns" flooded the ED department, trailed by cops, paramedics, and pissed off or scared relatives.

One of the superstitions of all ED employees is never to utter aloud, "Now it's quiet here." Even if two-thirds of the beds in the ED are empty and made with clean sheets, and it's so quiet that you can hear a fly buzz, under no circumstances should you say, "Now it's quiet here." Out of ignorance, I broke this rule a few times, blurting out, "Now it's quiet here," and everyone hissed at me: "Hey Peter, why are you saying THAT?!"

This is because, like a tornado unexpectedly swooping in on a peaceful village, changing it beyond recognition, the "yellow gowns zone" transforms the ED. One moment it's quiet and calm, and the next all the beds are taken; the clean white sheets are stained with blood and dirt; the air is poisoned with the stench of feces, vomit, and urine; the police and psych technicians are pacifying one agitated "yellow gown," while doctors and nurses are administering life-saving medicine to another who has overdosed.

DR. DJ

Working in ED opened a lot of new things for me. In a way, I started to pay much more attention to the physiological aspect of drug and alcohol addiction. I discovered how and why drugs and alcohol affect not only our psyche but the body.

Furthermore, while working in ED, I suddenly discovered a magical world of… American music! One of the doctors, Michael R., holding a senior administrative position in the department, offered me a free desk with a computer in the Administrator's office. I had an opportunity to spend part of the day inside the "yellow gown" zone and the rest working on a computer in this quiet office, alongside Dr. Michael.

Soon, I learned that Dr. Michael was a radio host at a music station, after which he decided to change the "record" in his life, graduated from medical school, and became a surgeon. Dr. Michael, however, did not bid farewell to music. In our shared office, while doing paperwork or working on the computer, he listened to radio shows on his cell phone, where old and new hits were played, critics discussed music pieces, and hosts interviewed musicians.

Once, as a familiar melody from my favorite group—the Doors—filled the air, I could not help myself and started singing along: "People are strange when you're a stranger…"

"When you're straaange…" Dr. Michael joined in.

We simultaneously looked at each other. By the expression on his face, I recognized that my eyes shone with the same enthusiastic excitement as his. It's like the gates had burst open. I started telling him about how in my youth in Russia I was a rock fanatic, learning all the song lyrics by heart from the Rolling Stones to Queen, singing them to my guitar, completely clueless to their meaning as I did not speak English. I related to him how as a teen I "was a traitor to my homeland," spending countless hours by the record store where I exchanged, bought, and sold Western rock—"smuggling," which resulted in the police arresting me a few times.

"There are not many changes in modern Russia today," I said. "Even though people have access to the internet and social media, under Putin's regime one still has to be a 'crazy' patriot, should still hate the West, and would certainly get into trouble if caught criticizing the government."

Leaning his chin on his hand, Dr. Michael carefully listened. He said that, in his opinion, any totalitarian regime is repulsive and contrary to human nature. We spoke about politics for a bit and then switched back to the topic of music. He asked me if I like the Kinks. I felt ashamed to acknowledge that, while I had heard of the band, I had never listened to any of their songs.

"Peter! How can this be? You don't know the Kinks?!" he interjected. "Here is your homework: listen to The Kinks, start with 'Lola' and 'Dead End Street.' Next Monday we will meet here and talk about what you heard. Also, take this journal 'Addictive Medicine' with you; the latest edition has some good stuff to read."

I started doing my "homework," reading the science journal "Addictive Medicine" while listening to the Kinks on my tablet. I waited impatiently for next Monday.

Dr. Michael had an amazing memory. Like a true rock fan, he recalled the album names and years of release, the concerts in Woodstock, Madison Square Garden, and Jones Beach, which he attended. "People are strange when you're a stranger…"

PHYSICIAN, HEAL THYSELF

Almost every day I discovered something new in my profession. I no longer tried to get the patients to like me, nor pretended that I was in recovery. I would rather try to understand them. In fact, I, too, was slowly undergoing profound change. I became more tolerant and less demanding of instant metamorphosis from anyone. I learned how not to judge.

This was a strange period in my life: I was growing professionally and, at the same time, I was experiencing a spiritual deadlock. All my efforts to better the lives of the patients didn't produce the results I expected; many of them used any means to remain in their misery.

Over time, I began to imagine drug addiction as a symbolic street—a long and winding road. Such a street exists in any city, village, or populated area. I called this street Misery Street. I first heard this name from a patient; he was a gifted poet, and one of his poems was called "Misery Street." You can find yourself on this street via various paths, each taking their own. One person might find themselves there due to a genetic predisposition to alcohol and drugs, while another came there under peer pressure, and someone else, out of curiosity. Of course, no one was going to linger on this street for long. For the first time in life, when raising a glass of wine or smoking the first blunt, no one does it to become a drug addict or an alcoholic. No one believed that it would happen to them. "It could happen to anyone else but not with me." O, ye.

Some lucky ones, having been on this street for a while, sooner or later managed to get off, while others stayed there forever. The longer a person remains on this street and the further along it he walks, the more chronically ill he becomes and the harder it is to get out of there.

Misery is one of the most common words in the lexicon of the addict: "misery loves company," "misery is my comfort zone," "misery seeks out the weak," and so on.

The fact is that any substance abuse treatment setting happens to be on Misery Street. There are youth gangs, domestic violence, sexually transmitted diseases, homelessness, the gun trade, prostitution, and prison—all of these are woven into the lives of the majority of the people there in one way or another. All moral vices flourish on Misery Street. Very seldom can you meet a drug addict who does not have psychiatric illness in addition to addiction. [8] Death is always looming around this Street.

Up until now, I considered myself a believer, a Christian. God has always been tantamount to goodness, truth, and beauty for me. But now I doubted the powers of his beauty and fairness. I doubted the power and goodness of God because I realized that evil is entrenched and ineradicable and will exist forever as long as this world exists. Human interventions, hospitals, and medicine are limited and can only reduce the stream of suffering, but not extinguish it.

How can we accept this world if it contains inextinguishable evil? How can you love a God who has created such a world?

These thoughts were so painful that I was overcome often by a sense of deep loneliness. My naïve childish faith in a good and gentle God had been shaken to the core.

WAR ZONE

As I already mentioned, the central hospital complex with the ED was located on the main boulevard in the Bronx, but our outpatient clinic, which was also part of a hospital, was located in a different place. It was in a high-crime, poor neighborhood. The so-called "war zone" or "ghetto."

Many stories are told about life in the ghetto by its residents, and many books have been written and movies made. I would probably not be telling readers anything new about this subject. I only want to give a few notes from my personal observations of the ghetto where I worked.

The majority of our patients said they grew up without fathers, fathers who were either in prison or elsewhere unknown, or who left one family to start another. It was not a surprise to hear female patients admit they had been engaged in prostitution since their early adolescence. Many of the patients had never worked legitimately or had no professional training.

Empty half-pint bottles of vodka and whisky are scattered near the curbs of the sidewalk. Although few cars are around, there are frequent car accidents, especially in the morning. That is because the drivers are suffering from terrible hangovers from drinking the night before. Empty bags from drugs can be found everywhere—on sidewalks, in parks, even in stores.

The neighborhood has a high rate of crime and violence. I remember one day sitting on the bench near the clinic during lunchtime and talking on my cell phone with Victoria. A big man was walking down the street towards me. He stopped next to me and pulled up his t-shirt. I saw the handle of a silver handgun sticking out from his belt. An icy chill ran down my spine. I thought that I won't get the chance to tell Vicky at last how much I love her. The man looked at me, scratched his belly, pulled his t-shirt down, and continued walking.

Patients in our clinic often spoke about shootings in the neighborhood. At least once a week, some patient would tell of a relative or friend being wounded in a recent shooting. At the beginning, I doubted all of these "war" stories. I suspected patients were exaggerating and dramatizing. But very often on my way to the clinic and on my way back, I saw streets blocked off by police tape and houses surrounded by cops. On the evening local TV news, I heard reports about new shootings, new victims, and new arrests at the very places I passed earlier.

There are a lot of churches, shelters and residential facilities, pantries, and suicide prevention agencies. Of course, there are also nightclubs, bars, discotheques, and liquor stores.

This is the "ghetto" façade, so to speak, something that catches one's eye.

Our clinic shared space on its premises with a community medical ambulatory clinic, where residents from the local area were treated. I had access to all patients' electronic charts, so I had the chance to see their lives from a medical point of view. What did I see? A whole bouquet of serious chronic diseases: from hypertension to diabetes, from asthma to cancer. Not only among the elderly but mostly among those in their forties. Or even thirties. Obesity, anemia, AIDS. An incredible number of people who suffered from schizophrenia, bipolar, and psychosis. And of course, drug and alcohol addiction.

THE CHILDREN OF THE GHETTO

Nearly half of those living in this ghetto were Black, which, in turn, was reflected in the racial composition of our patients. Generations received treatment at our substance abuse clinic. First, parents used to get treatment here, and now it was time for their children to do so, too.

The Black patients didn't want to have anything to do with me and right away asked our director to change counselors because I, as a white man, could never understand a Black person. However, the director of our clinic didn't always agree to their demands.

Most of them were young Black men between the ages of twenty and twenty-five. These young men not only smoked grass but peddled it as well. They sold grass or cocaine, standing on the corner or next to the bodegas until undercover cops would bust them. Then, as a rule, the court put them on probation and mandated them to treatment. Then another seller would take their spot immediately.

Of course, these guys came into the clinic already pissed—they were ashamed. Such tough guys who weren't afraid of anything were forced into treatment. In addition, they didn't think of themselves as addicts because "almost everybody smokes ganja in the ghetto."

Some of them were pressured into giving up smoking pot, but they kept selling it. They came to us "for treatment" with expensive leather jackets, thick gold chains on their chest, and gold teeth—they explained to me it was very cool and prestigious in their ghetto to have white gold caps on one's teeth. Almost all of them were already chronic drug users. They smoked pot from the age of eleven or twelve. If they stopped smoking, then they'd begin to drink vodka and whiskey heavily.

They didn't hide their disrespect for me. They'd grown up on the street and were street smart, while I was book smart. There's a huge gap between the books and the streets.

I remember one of these men, James. He was a very spiteful man who looked at everybody askance, sticking out his lower jaw.

"Yeah, I smoke grass. But I don't sell it anymore, you understand, doc? It's a big step for me. Selling weed is my profession, my bread and butter. You should be praising me instead of shoving that piece of paper in my face that says I'm 'dirty.' Sorry, doc, but you have no clue about real life."

James once mentioned in conversation that he used to work for a park landscaping company and he'd liked the job. I decided to spend an extra hour with him: I called an agency that helps ex-convicts get jobs. I praised James to them, saying that he was a landscaping expert and an excellent gardener. They offered James an interview—one company was hiring landscapers right away. I promised James that I'd help him with his resume as well.

James glanced suspiciously at me, muttered, and then left. He came back and knocked on the door of my office unexpectedly fifteen minutes later.

"My mom was a prostitute who smoked crack. I never knew my dad. My grandma raised me. Whenever I went to my mom's place, there were always men—her clients. My mother hated me, said she got pregnant against her will because she was drunk. When I was thirteen, my two older cousins molested me."

James told me all of this as he sat in the chair staring at the wall in front of him and didn't even wipe the large tears that were rolling down his high cheekbones.

"When I first got out of jail and went home, my mother wasn't even happy for me. She was with a new fucker. She didn't have any photos of me in the apartment."

I've heard such stories—with minor variations—many times. Even if some of these guys didn't open up to me, too ashamed, I already understood what kind of family and childhood they had come from.

I once had to facilitate a group session where only three patients showed up. All three were black and mandated for treatment, on parole or probation. They either continued to smoke pot, drink, or sell drugs. I got on each of their cases and threatened to call probation if they wouldn't change. Of course, they couldn't stand me. In addition, I could barely understand their language because of the special slang and jargon of the drug dealers in their ghetto. Now I had to run a group session with them for three hours!

Before the start of the group, I left the building for a breath of fresh air. I looked up at the gray clouds in the sky. "How can I handle three hours of being embarrassed? God, give me the strength."

The session started. They began by attacking me with verbal insults. Then I said, "Okay, guys. You don't like me. According to you, I'm a racist. I'm book smart. I'm a man. Do you think it would be better if, instead of me, your counselor was a black woman with a great ass? Would you think about treatment then?"

They got caught off-guard, shot me a look, and then smiled.

Many years passed. Since that day, I've probably conducted a thousand group sessions. But not one could compare with that unforgettable one when these three opened up. They argued among themselves, shared their secret dreams, laughed, and even cried.

I also interjected my two cents to their conversation. I

objected or agreed, completely forgetting that I don't understand their slang. I understood everything! Without a doubt.

Leaving the room after the session, James (he was also among them) gave me a friendly slap on the shoulder:

"Respect, doc! You're a better counselor than any big ass Black shawty!"

"I WANT YOU TO SPELL SOMETHING FOR ME, JIM"

During the days when I worked in ED and shared the office with DJ Doctor Michael, I found out a lot of new things about American music, which is generally performed by black musicians.

Doctor Michael, as it turned out, was a large fan of not just classic rock, but other music genres: reggae, spirituals, blues. Until now I had of course known the names of Jimi Hendrix, Bob Marley, Ray Charles—the stars known around the world. But I had never heard of the less famous, but no less remarkable performers, like James Brown, Sam Cook, Ted Hawkins, and Dillinger. Thanks to Dr. Michael, I discovered a whole new layer of music culture, which I had no clue even existed.

There was a period when during our brief office breaks in ED we completely switched over to traditional African-American music. At times we sat in the office together hours at a time at adjoining desks, not speaking at all because we had so much work to do. Our phones and beepers would not quiet down. We both worked at computers, banged on our keyboards, made calls, and answered calls. After a few tense hours, Dr. Michael suddenly stretched in his seat, straightening his numb back. Then he would get up and close the door of our office. A thin, sneaky smile played on his lips.

For me, it was the signal for a music break!

"Peter, my dear fellow, I want you to hear this now. Listen and tell me your opinion."

He would then find a song on his cell phone on YouTube.

"Hey, Jim. Jim, just a minute y'all,
I want to ask you somethin'.
I want you to spell somethin' for me, Jim . . .
I've got cocaine runnin' around my brain . . ."

Dillinger was singing, appearing on the mobile screen.

"Wow, Doctor! I like it!" I exclaimed.

Doctor Michael shook his head, beaming from joy.

And suddenly the ghetto would burst into our quiet workspace, buried under paperwork, crammed with computers, phones, and a copy machine. Ghetto, which I knew a bit, was not painful, sick, and cruel, but mischievous, simple-hearted, and full of fun.

"I just want you to spell New York, Jim.
We alright. I'm gonna go ahead, man.
N-E-W Y-O-R-K. That's New York, man..."

Music breaks were, of course, great, but the relationship between ghetto inhabitants and police were devoid of any fun. None at all. Almost daily, one black patient or another would come in and resentfully tell us how he was stopped for no reason by cops, who questioned and searched him. Every time I hear the swearing and curses of our black patients against cops (mostly white ones), I thought that this can't go on for long—sooner or later the temperature of anger will rise to the boiling point and there will be an explosion.

Indeed, soon enough the murder of George Floyd would take place followed by unrest. Currently, the topic of race remains one of the most painful in the U.S.

PART FOUR

KEEP GOING, STUDENT!

A new social worker was hired in our outpatient clinic. Tracy was a young woman, around thirty. She had recently graduated from Fordham University, with a diploma and a license, and started working in her new profession. We developed a somewhat friendly relationship.

Often social workers or psychologists look at addiction counselors from above—the LMSW license is above that of an addiction counselor, and there are more job responsibilities, better knowledge, and higher compensation. However, Tracy was completely devoid of any snobbery. She had the makings of a good clinician despite her lack of clinical experience, and she possessed theoretical knowledge, having just graduated from the University. By contrast, I had a good amount of clinical experience by that time.

Tracy and I rarely spoke about our personal lives. I only knew that she was a single mother of Caribbean origin and that her seven-year-old daughter attended elementary school; a few times after work I dropped her off at home in Bushwick, where she rented an apartment in a private house.

In the summer, when Tracy wore a short-sleeved blouse, I noticed on her dark arms three thin light strips of scars—usually such scars are left after wrist-cutting attempts. I never asked her about these scars. It is possible that they had something to do with her single mother status; maybe even her choice to be a social worker was not by chance. It just so happens that the workers in substance abuse and psychiatric clinics, child protective agencies, foster care agencies, and other similar places of employment, are usually those who themselves had their share of grief, and not just random people.

Once, during lunch, Tracy and I walked down the alley and talked about something.

"Man, why don't you go to university for a master's program?" she asked suddenly.

"University?"

"Yes. You're a sharp guy, but to become a cool shrink you need theoretical knowledge. Why don't you try for Fordham? It is a private university, and fairly easy to get into, but it's not cheap and not easy to study. I am sure you can do it."

"Do you think so?"

I recalled how foolishly I dropped out of a college in Russia, when I was in my last year, and never got my diploma. It would have come in handy now. Still, inside I was grateful to Tracy for this idea. I thought about this more than once myself, that an addiction counselor certificate won't be enough.

After my acquaintance with Tracy, I was fully convinced that my theoretical knowledge in psychology, psychotherapy, and sociology was rather limited. I understood that I needed to study further, but had no idea where to begin.

I involuntarily recalled those days long ago when I studied in the substance abuse school while working as a security guard in the Time Warner Building. I remembered how once I left my post, following the students who were passing by the Time Warner building, and ended up in front of Fordham University. How I sat there, on the granite slab, near the statue of Saint Francis, and had strange visions of my future.

"Okay, it's decided! I am applying to Fordham. Thank you, my dear."

"Keep going, student!" I said to myself when I got off the train at Columbus Circle in Manhattan. Pedestrians were pushing me around like a ball on my way down the street from the underground. I passed a Starbucks, the Time Warner skyscraper, benches with sleeping homeless people, police horses, and yellow cabs with advertising signs; I walked past maple trees, sycamores, security guards, hotel doormen, and fat, panting men in overcoats crawling out of limos, young women in sable coats following close behind them . . . and, crossing the street, I approached the ultimate goal of my 10-minute journey: the Fordham University building.

Here at the university, I didn't doubt—as I'd done years before, at the substance abuse school—that I'd wound up at the right address or the right classroom. Students here didn't curse during the lectures and didn't test the patience of their professors; they didn't jump up from their desks in order to engage in a theater performance, or stun those present with revelation after revelation. This was a different world, and a different atmosphere reigned here of workshops, serious reading, and intellectual disputes.

Understandably, I had never studied in American colleges and universities and did not know how the process worked. I presumed that, like in Russia, the professors will dictate lectures, assign homework daily, and grade it, followed by a class discussion.

However, everything happened quite differently here. We got homework reading assignments, but we rarely discussed them afterward, and we learned new material during the following lecture. I liked this new system of learning. No one inquired whether I was reading the homework or not. Obviously, I never opened any textbooks. I went to the movies with Vicky after work, walked around the city with her, and kept buying archaic vinyl records in Greenwich Village, replenishing my music collection. Vicky reminded me sometimes that it wouldn't hurt to read the college's books from time to time, but I saw no need for this. I am smart anyway. There was nothing easier and more pleasurable than to study at an American university for a master's degree!

Suddenly, in the middle of a semester, we got a test in every class, which shocked me. I did not know the answers to a significant amount of questions, and did not even understand what it was about: Piaget's Theory? Erickson's Theory? Bowlby's Theory? Who were these guys? Only then did it dawn on me that I was supposed to have acquainted myself with all those details independently since the professors only gave general knowledge and some guidance during lectures. Obviously, I got "Fs" and "Cs" in my midterms. My real studies began only after having learned this lesson.

After more time passed, I realized that the university students fell into two relatively distinct groups. The first was the "worker bees." These were the ones who had already been working at different social service agencies, medical centers, and hospitals for some time, and who had families and children. They needed their degree in order to move up the career ladder. Employers would often pay to send these workers to study hard, put their nose to the grindstone, and receive a diploma—all for (only) $70,000! These people didn't have time for chit-chat; they raced from work to the university and then, at half-past nine, once their final class was finished, they'd go home. The majority of them lived in the Bronx or Brooklyn, or Harlem, so that it would take them at least an hour on the subway since many express trains don't run at night. And they would still need to prepare for class the next day and read a hundred pages in the textbook. And study for an exam in another class. And, in addition to all of the above, a spouse would be waiting at home, wanting to talk, wanting for affection. Their child—not wishing to study in school, but waiting for care and warmth. On top of all these circumstances and concerns is the added burden of an internship: twenty hours a week of unpaid work in a medical facility or social agency. In short, from morning until night, the tick-tock of a clock in their head warns them loudly, "Hurry, hurry, you'll be late!"

These students often reminded me of cargo planes waiting on the runway. They were always ready for takeoff, and when they sat in the auditorium, they would look exhaustedly at their watches. As soon as the professor announced the end of the lesson, the auditorium turned into an aerodrome and—laden with bags heavy with textbooks, notebooks, empty plastic plates washed quickly after lunch break at work, folders filled with various papers—these airplanes quickly left the auditorium. Vrrrr-vrrr-vroom!

The second group of students wasn't that of worker bees or cargo planes, but instead comprised beautiful butterflies that collect pollen in a meadow of pleasure and comfort. This beautiful fluttering flock consisted mostly of out-of-state white girls from middle-class families. Once they graduated from their small-town colleges with degrees in sociology or art, they decided to get a master's in social work and dedicate their lives to the less fortunate—those who had fallen on hard times or suffered from mental illness. I honestly don't know what motivated them to take such an exalted path. If they possessed a special fervor for sacrifice or any particular compassion for others, it wasn't noticeable to me.

Most likely, the reasons for it were not spiritual, but rather practical: Without vivid talent or inclination toward other professions such as programming or medicine, without outstanding artistic ability, these women were forced to choose a profession that was more popular and easier to get: that of a social worker. Actually, I related to them because I myself did not have any talents or significant skills for either science or art.

And one more factor played an important role in their choice: Their parents remained home in the suburbs of Minnesota and Pennsylvania, and the young women up-up-and-awayed on a plane to glistening, bustling New York City.

Parents significantly paid not only for their children's education but also for the cost of living in NYC, the "capital of the world," where there are many bars, restaurants, discos, and nightclubs. Freeee-dom! The parents paid for everything. But as Jessica, Marilyn, and even stingy Kathy confessed to me, all the same, the money wasn't even close to being sufficient. Money melted away like snow on the sun, so it was necessary for them to take out loans and obtain a line of credit, not for classes, but for personal expenses. (Any such "student life" loans are given out by banks at high-interest rates, and the interest starts to accrue immediately.)

I recently came across an article in the *New York Times* about how U.S. intelligence agencies uncovered some Russian spies. As reported in the newspaper, Russian intelligence officers were engaged in financial espionage in New York and they tried to recruit American students into their Russian spy network: "American students, contrary to our expectations, proved to be very closed off and difficult to make contact with. In order to recruit them, it's been necessary to spend a great deal more time and money than expected," reported one spy to his boss in Moscow (The FBI had intercepted their emails and phone conversations.)

I suspect that this unfortunate spy was simply trying to extract some more money from his bosses in Moscow, playing them for fools. Or maybe he didn't try to recruit the right female students? Perhaps he referred not to the flying fairies, but to the workhorses who were burdened with family, work, internships, and study. Were they the ones he couldn't recruit?

Students in the U.S. are quite open and responsive. Sometimes, I would say, they are too open.

I remember during one seminar in my alma mater, paired with the sultry Angela, I practiced "assessment during the patient's first visit." I had the role of the shrink, she, the patient. As was customary, I asked Angela in a heartfelt manner which problems in her life she considered the most serious at the time. Angela never wore a bra to these night seminars. She had amazing, full breasts, with a shiny gold necklace on her tanned skin. After class, which finished a quarter after ten, she was always in a hurry somewhere. I am sure it was not to the library.

Licking her thickly painted lips, Angela moaned, "You ask what problems I have? Oh, doctor, you have no idea how badly I want to fuck…"

And still, I am wrong because I say all of this with irony. After some time passes, these flying fairies, having received their diplomas, will go to work in social service agencies and medical facilities where they'll face real human suffering. For many of them, this will prove a big challenge. Not all of them will be able to deal with it. Some will leave the field forever and attempt to forget "the nightmare," having decided that it would be better to deal with paperwork, numbers, or computer programs than with unhappy people with a broken fate. Others will meet this challenge with honor and respect. They discover wonderful human qualities within themselves and acquire proficient clinical skills. They learn to deeply understand people and life.

Thanks to this profession, the same thing happened to me.

I learned about another America: a student America. And I became a real expert. Now I could apply theoretical knowledge into my practice in the clinic immediately. Knowledge makes life easier.

Inexhaustibly energetic, I wanted to treat everyone. Everyone around me—the entire world—had an emergency requiring the attention of a young shrink. Patients, colleagues at work, neighbors—everyone needed psychotherapy.

My dear Vicky was the most difficult of all of my "unofficial patients." She took the main blow of my psychotherapy practice. I treated her everywhere we went, no matter where we were, and during any time (whether in the subway, eating supper, or in bed before, during, and after sex). I am surprised to this day how she didn't leave me by "quitting her treatment" then and there.

"First-semester student's syndrome" was quickly progressing. I gradually developed a new way of looking at people. I now noticed one or another psychiatric disorder in everyone I saw. Not only in patients. Everyone around me seemed to be a "walking diagnosis." Of course, I recognized every psych disorder in myself, as well.

OF SEX, ROMANCE, AND AIDS

RED STRIPE

Earlier, I talked of the narrow red stripe that appears on the white stick during a toxicology screening. But there's another fate-altering red line. I'm speaking of the HIV test they give in some substance abuse clinics.

The test is simple: A counselor gives the patient a plastic stick; the patient then puts the end of the stick in his mouth. (An HIV virus can be determined through saliva, though results are more accurate and more detailed with a blood test.) Then this stick is dipped into a small tube containing a special liquid.

Complete silence descends. Dead silence. Both the counselor and the patient watch the white plastic stick in the tube very carefully. Though they may engage in some small talk during this time, their eyes are fixed on the tester stick. Will a red line appear? You know, some unpleasant thoughts come to mind at this time. Recollections of parties with booze and mischievous gals. All past flirtations and amorous adventures run through the mind in their dirtiest, most obnoxious form. How do I know all this? That's right—I tested myself for HIV. I closed the door, took out the test stick, and made the sign of the cross. "God, help me . . ."

In my observation, men are more nervous than women waiting for the results of the test, probably because men are more promiscuous by nature. They're Casanovas. Even though men are considered the stronger sex, men are weaker in their psyche. Mental stress is very difficult for us. Our psyche is so sensitive and vulnerable. Only a minute passes and the man, without lifting his eyes off the stick, begins to breathe harder, puff out his cheeks, and fidget in his chair. During this minute, he is undoubtedly uttering an oath: "Never again, no way, will I have sex with anyone but my dear wife."

Yes, this test has tremendous significance, I tell you.

Over several years, I tested not only our patients but anyone who wanted to be tested. Let's say all of a sudden, a man "from the streets" wants to know his HIV status. He'd come to our clinic, register, sign the required paperwork, and "mount the scaffold" to take the test.

That's when I first came across this phenomenon: sex with a partner who is known to be infected with HIV. Sex without a condom. For example, a young woman came to my office and asked to be tested. I opened the package for the test, then took the testing tube out of the box while I was asking her the standard questions about her marital status, her sexual history, and so on.

"Officially, doctor, I'm divorced. I live with a man who has AIDS. He gives me money and buys me gifts. Here, look at this bracelet—it's gold. Look at my iPod—it's the latest one. He gave me these last week. We do have unprotected sex, yes, fuck without a condom. I know, I know. It's dangerous, and I can be exposed. That's why I came to you to get checked. I'll be careful from now on and take this seriously. Give me the stick and . . . how do I put it in? In my mouth? Like this?"

I've come across such women so often that I am no longer surprised by their confessions. By the way, lectures on how to prevent the spread of HIV are offered even in elementary schools in New York City.

The surprising truth is that none of these women's tests came up with positive results. Not one test I conducted over several years on women having unprotected sex with HIV-infected men. By some miracle, none had contracted the virus.

I have no explanation for this, and I have struggled with the question: Why can someone contract the virus after spending just one pleasant night with an unfamiliar man or woman they met on a cruise ship for example (as happened with a friend of mine), while others who practically sell their bodies for money and gold bling, while perfectly aware of the risk and possible consequences, can come out unscathed?

But somehow it happens just like this.

There was a box of condoms on one of the shelves in my office. Like a kind of medical Santa Claus, after every test, I gave a moralistic speech and always offered free condoms as a gift. As a rule, men proudly refused. But women took them greedily and without hesitation.

Female condoms were very popular with women. One of my patients worked for an escort service: occasionally she came into my office and took almost my entire weekly stock in one fell swoop, for herself and her friends. Could I refuse her? Of course not.

WORKING WITH THE LGBTQ COMMUNITY

In Fordham, I took a class called "Working with the LGBTQ Community." I should say at least a few words about this class. This class was led by a professor named David Koch, an openly gay American Jew. He was very emotional, but a discerning and wise professor. He told us about his personal life story, or rather, the personal story of his spouse. The spouse's whole family had turned away from him when they found out he was a homosexual. Only after many years, when his spouse built a career and achieved a certain social standing in society, was he finally invited to a family gathering. He came to his relatives and during the party, while looking at a photo album with old pictures, bitterly discovered that his face was carefully cut out of every photo, starting from early childhood.

The majority of students who took this class were gay, lesbian, bisexual, or otherwise LGBTQ. There were only two straight students, myself and another guy from another Eastern European country. I don't know why he took this elective class. He was an explicit homophobe, although he did not consider himself as such, and moreover he was convinced that he was an ardent defender of all gays. He had no doubt that homosexuality was a severe psychiatric disorder and pathology which had no cure. He voiced this conviction on the first day when students were introducing themselves and getting to know each other. He continued to defend this view about homosexuality as a psychiatric disorder during the whole semester, and the knowledge he gained during the semester did not change his point of view. LGBTQ students were annoyed by his speeches, to say the least. Of course, they called him a confirmed homophobe from medieval times. But he never got offended, considering them severely psychologically ill. I can't imagine how Professor Koch must have gnashed his teeth while reading his midterm and final papers and what grade he gave him—"A" or "B"? "Should I give him a 'C'? Or maybe an 'F'? F...fucking idiot!" I suspect Professor Koch thought this while reading the papers of this strange and self-righteous student.

I explained during our introductions that the LGBTQ class was not just a personal but a professional interest for me. This was true because then I was interning in the outpatient drug clinic, which was located in Greenwich Village, and many of the patients there were LGBTQ.

I want to mention the LGBTQ patients in that clinic because it is relevant to the topic of our story. In general, these were gay men, 25-40 years old. The majority of them used crystal meth. Crystal meth is an artificial stimulant which, in addition to everything else, greatly heightens sexual activity.

In the process of getting to know this group of people, I came to realize that intimacy plays a significant role in gay life. The high importance of intimate relationships explains the popularity of crystal meth among gay men.

During my internship at the clinic, I saw very few gay patients who had long-term success with stopping their usage of crystal meth. They relapsed more often than the patients who used other types of drugs. In my year of interning in that clinic, probably out of twenty LGBTQ patients who used crystal meth, I remembered just one who stopped and remained clean for a year (I hope he is still clean). For the others, crystal meth relapses carried severe consequences, including ending up in psych wards due to psychosis.

From the gay patients, I found out a lot about societal pressure, which comes in various forms. In addition, inside the LGBTQ community of NYC, as it turned out, all is not so smooth; there are all types of abuse based on race and age, sexual exploitation, male prostitution, etc.

I also was shocked by the high level of HIV/AIDS among LGBTQ male patients. I will not be exaggerating when I say that every third if not second of those using crystal meth was infected with HIV or had AIDS. Yes, the AIDS epidemic, which erupted in the USA at the end of the seventies and the beginning of the eighties, fortunately, has passed. Medicine has been developed to help those who are already infected, as well as for prevention. A lot of educational and preventive work has been done, and the fight against AIDS has lost its acuteness and relevance, especially given the background of other epidemics currently prevalent in the US.

Alas, this does not apply to the gay users of crystal meth, particularly in New York. The spread of HIV/AIDS in their community is still just as rampant as decades ago.

POETRY OF DON JUAN

Juan was a poet. He was a strong, broad-shouldered Dominican man of about fifty, with a round, fleshy face and large dark-brown eyes.

He stood before an audience of patients in the large hall in our clinic in the Bronx; he was holding a piece of paper with a new poem in his hand. He began to recite, waving his free hand in rhythm:

A walk down Misery Street,
A place where people meet.
You see some nod, many sob.
What is this place? I ask God.

Having read the last line, he grew silent and, looking up from his sheet of paper, glanced expectantly in front of him.

"Bravo! Bravo!" exploded the hall.

Juan cast his eyes down shyly. Suddenly, this fifty-year-old man began to smile, as if he was the happiest child in the whole world.

I remember well the day when Juan first crossed the threshold of my office. He walked in confidently and then gave me a searching look. He asked that he and his girlfriend, who was in the waiting room, be tested for HIV.

"I have AIDS, that I know," he said outright. "I've had the

virus for fifteen years. I want to send this information to the Infectious Diseases Department of the hospital today. That's why I need to do the test right now."

"I understand." I slowly started to unpack the test kits and the boxes with the test tubes.

Juan had recently been released from prison, where he had served time for robbing a store. He had firmly decided to get off drugs and start living "right."

As he told me, he'd become infected with HIV in Nuremberg, Germany, where he had once served as a U.S. Marine.

"We American soldiers had our pockets full of money back then. That's why the German women loved us." He smiled. "Nuremberg, like any city in Germany, was full of brothels, and our whole platoon would visit them. I received this medal in a brothel."

"And what about your girlfriend?" I asked, making the final preparations for the test.

"Well, here's her story. She's a nice chick. It's true, she smokes a little weed. We've lived together for a few months."

"I hope you've been using condoms?"

Juan shook his head.

Soon afterward, a young twenty-three-year-old, light-skinned, slim female, with long legs and large gold earrings, came into the room. She looked like a supermodel.

I explained to them what to do, how to put the stick in their mouths, and told them the results would be available in a few minutes.

When they had completed the tests and given me back the sticks, Juan suggested to his girlfriend, "Let's go have a smoke."

"Let's go," she agreed.

Left alone in the room, I stared blankly at the two white sticks in the test tubes. A thin light red line appeared slowly on one of them. Juan's stick. Actually, there was no other result to expect from that stick. He himself had admitted having AIDS for many years.

But what about his pretty woman? What if it suddenly

turned out she was infected? Stupid! Absolutely stupid! What did she need him for? What would happen if the test comes back positive? Do I really have to be the one to tell her the terrible news? I'll have to comfort her and calm her? Express sorrow and empathy? A surgeon who should inform the family that a patient has died during an operation must experience a similar feeling.

They knocked at the door, Juan and his girlfriend. I exhaled with great relief and told her that she was doing just fine, with no signs of the virus.

"Everything's okay, miss. See, this is your stick and there's no red line. But in the future, please be careful. You know that unprotected sex . . . there are precautions, condoms . . ."

She didn't argue. She smiled and nodded. I concluded that my words had gone in one pretty little ear and out the other.

At one point I turned to Juan. He walked carefully up to the table, and holding his breath, looked at his stick with the vivid thick red line. He had hoped. After fifteen years, he still had hope! Even knowing the virus does not leave the body.

That's how deeply hope is rooted within us! Hope will not die, even in the face of all common sense! Even if we know that something is impossible, even if we get used to it, even if we accept it . . . still . . .

It's like this. Never give up on a person and bury them before his time. It's better to believe that all is not lost. To spare him.

Juan glanced at me. He looked confused. I guessed that he was ashamed of the fact that someone now saw his dashed hope and the disappointment that followed. He nodded with a deep sigh:

"Ah, there are no miracles on Misery Street."

CRIME AND PUNISHMENT

WAR ON DRUGS

One day, I picked up an empty heroin bag from the sidewalk near the clinic. I put it in my pocket and decided to go for a walk with it. Just for the sake of curiosity. Try it yourself if you wish. Then you will recount the icy chill that runs up your spine when a police car drives past you.

Drug users carry these—full—bags around the clock. They hide them in their socks, in their jacket lining, and under the seat in their car. Very adventurous guys.

In the context of current laws, they're all criminals who have committed the offense of "drug possession." That is, having purchased the drug and placed it in his pocket, a person finds himself on the wrong side of the law. If, for example, a crack pipe is found in his pocket, this is irrefutable evidence that also leads to a charge under the heading "Possession of Drug Paraphernalia." An active addict violates the law daily over the course of many years. That is why he has to be constantly vigilant, maintain an outward calm, avoid police checkpoints, and watch out everywhere in the city for men who look suspicious: "Could they be undercover?" The paranoid feelings set in.

With the looming purchase of another pill or bag, the drug user already feels the high before the high, in anticipation. At the same time, there is a vague and distant moral unease. He still remembers the oath he gave to his wife, how he promised himself, how he swore on the health of his child, and how he swore on the Bible or the Torah. Still, he returns to the dealer yet again to buy junk. He pays his money and hides his purchased goods. Then he attempts to tuck away his guilty conscience in the far corner of his heart.

This inner conflict and paranoia about being busted are the cause of irritability, the constant defensive and belligerent attitude of an active drug user toward everyone, most especially toward those before whom he feels most guilty.

If you paid attention to the aforementioned scene, there are two crimes the supposed drug user has committed, one moral and one legal. In other words, he is twice as guilty. However, if the moral crime is on his conscience, then the legal one is very conditional. Because moral laws are immutable and eternal, while legal ones are changeable, authorities redraw these latter one way or the other, due to various reasons—political, financial, social, etc.

There is no need to go far for examples of this. A hundred years ago, America implemented Prohibition. A person desiring to have an alcoholic beverage, forbidden by the government, went to his bootlegger (the alcohol dealer) and not to the store, committing the same felony as someone buying heroin or crack from a drug dealer today.

Moralism and religious intolerance propelled the movement towards goodness. "A real Christian has to work hard and care for his family; alcohol is from the devil." It is well-known that good intentions pave the road to hell. During Prohibition, the bootleggers' mafia became very powerful while the state treasury became more impoverished. We also know how this fight with the "demon" ended. Prohibition became defunct, and alcohol was legalized; the mafia had to look for another area to operate, while the state treasury, ravaged by the Great Depression, saw an inflow of billions of dollars from the taxes collected on sold beverages with alcoholic content of various proof.

Today, the existing rules seem reasonable and obvious. Today, a person coming into a liquor store for a bottle of vodka seems to us like a regular customer, the same as one entering a shoe store or an electronics store, but the one going to a drug dealer to buy an ounce of weed or a bag of heroin is viewed as a drug addict, committing a criminal offense.

But for us clinicians, working in various medical settings, there is no difference whether the person developed an addiction from "legal" alcohol or "illegal" cocaine. We see the patient in a different light—not through a prism of criminal law, the way prosecutors or judges do, but through a prism of clinical symptoms.

And what do we see? We see a monstrous destruction of the whole human body, caused by "legal" alcohol. We see cirrhosis of the liver, heart failure, alcoholic epilepsy, delirium tremens, diabetes, depression and suicide—all brought on by alcohol.

How many crimes are committed due to inebriation by legal alcohol! Spousal or child beating, auto accidents, fights, rapes, malicious disorderly behavior, theft, vandalism, involuntary manslaughter...

There is no need to go far for examples. I remember the monster into which my own kind-hearted father turned after an emptied bottle of vodka. In the morning, after sobering up, he would be ashamed of yesterday's behavior, tormented by remorse, and could not look into my mother's eyes or mine.

And alcohol is legal!

Today it has become evident that the War on Drugs America declared in the late 60s and early 70s has since suffered a crushing defeat.

It is known that the War on Drugs was a government response to the growing addiction triggered by the veterans of the Vietnam War returning back to the US addicted to opiates. The War on Drugs was initially conceived as a broad, full-blown measure, including, on one side, comprehensive treatment for drug addiction, and on the other, harsher penalties for narco-traffickers. However, at some point, the punitive measures started to dominate. The government began encouraging excessive use of force, militarizing the police, and significantly toughening up the punishment for drug-related crimes. As a result, the world of addicts, already connected with crimes, was criminalized even more. Jail cells started to quickly fill up with thousands of new "criminals."

If we compare the drug policy in the US and Western Europe or our neighboring Canada, we can easily find a lot of differences. There, the attitude towards drug addiction has always been softer and more liberal. For example, in most of Western Europe marijuana has been legal for a long time. For as long as decades, programs have existed for exchanging "dirty" needles and disposable syringes for "clean" ones. So-called Safer Injection Stations have arisen, where drug addicts can peacefully use clean needles, cotton balls, and everything else needed; nurses at these stations even teach them how to shoot dope to reduce the risk of abscesses and STDs.

In opposition to this, America, having declared the War on Drugs, turned again to the path of high morality; the old puritan moral of intolerance took the upper hand, which once upon a time became the main engine for Prohibition: "A real Christian has to work hard and care for his family; drugs are from the devil." Even while admitting that drug addiction is a psychiatric disorder, the U.S. government and our society still continued to demand total sobriety from the drug user. "You're sick, okay; get treatment and get clean. We don't want to see you dirty. We want to see you clean." This is what we want. The drug user also wants the same, by the way, but, alas, it is not happening. It happens for some, but not for everyone, and not right away.[9] The time has come when we need to admit this, and make more realistic demands on drug users, instead of demands stemming from our well-intended utopian wishes.

It is remarkable that Western Europe and Canada do not have an opiate epidemic as we in the US have now. Heroin and opiates pills exist in Europe and Canada, just like the ones in the US. Drug users exist there as well, but no epidemic of opiate overdoses.

Decriminalization and legalization of drugs would lead to addicts (those who have already become such and those who are in the process) not having to hide from us; for at least a bit, they would come out of the shadows and become more approachable for medical help. There would be more points of contact, and everyone would benefit from such convergence. By the way, the jails would become less crowded. And we would view drug addicts not as criminals like we do today. It is time to develop a fundamentally new approach to drug addiction on the federal level.

Right now, the process of marijuana's decriminalization and legalization is ongoing. It is moving slowly, creaking, and in many states looks like it will drag on for years, if not decades. I am not even talking about other, bolder measures, such as organizing Safer Injection Stations. Sad to say, but even, for now, the majority of states continue to exercise measures of the century-old fashion: for example, it is still forbidden there to have programs for the exchange of "dirty" needles for "clean" ones, and after saving addicts from overdosing, the police take them straight from the hospital to the police precinct to open criminal cases against them.

THE CRIMINAL WORLD

Going from one extreme to the next is obviously not recommended. Decriminalization and legalization of drugs will not lead to the complete disappearance of criminal offenses.

Any addiction by its very nature changes a person's personality, disrupts his psyche, and destroys his morality. How many times, while dealing with an actively using patient, I am seized by irritation, dislike, and anger towards him! Sometimes I look at him, sitting across from me, and think to myself: "My God, what a lying, callous, insolent man! How dark his soul is! He believes that he is allowed everything. Someone like him will not hesitate to commit any crime. Why is he trampling the earth and poisoning the air with his existence? He won't be fixed by medication, therapy, prison—nothing."

Then he disappears somewhere and you let out a sigh of relief. "Thank God, I won't see that scumbag again."

And then you meet him again, in say five years. He has been clean for a long time, working or studying, and he's now a family man—an adequate person, who has nothing in common with the one you once knew and couldn't stand. Upon parting, he'll also thank you for all your efforts, which, it turns out, helped him a lot.

But, as we've already mentioned, not all drug users immediately achieve such a goal. Some of them require years to get off Misery Street. Others stay there forever, committing one crime after another (mostly because they need money for drugs). That is why the world of drug addicts is so close to the world of criminals or, more precisely, makes up a significant part of the criminal world.

Murder and cruel acts inevitably accompany drug trafficking. Drug dealers fight among themselves and with the law enforcement agencies. The word "war" in this case is not a metaphor.

I remember, during my shift in ED, two men entered, impeccably dressed in dark suits, shirts, and ties, with neat haircuts. They looked so out of place here. Were they university professors or Wall Street brokers? Or perhaps they came to visit their colleague in ED. I tried to guess who they were.

In five minutes, the loudspeaker announced for the Trauma Team to urgently go to ED. Such announcements, when the Trauma Team is urgently called to ED, are not heard often, only in the case of a patient in critical condition, with a serious, life-threatening injury being brought.

Shortly, into the special, pre-op ward, where the walls and doors were made of glass, they brought in a Caucasian man, around thirty-five. There were two bloody bandages on his face. After the surgeons, the "Wall Street brokers"—they were FBI agents followed in. A few policemen already guarded the entrance to that ward.

Nurses, psych technicians, and clerks could not hide their curiosity, and under any pretext they walked past that ward, peeping through the wide glass doors to see what was going on. I also walked by a few times, appearing busy, squeezing between the doctors and cops. I looked at the patient lying there.

I soon found out from colleagues that this patient was a high-ranking drug dealer. Competitors had put two bullets into his head; one crushed his jaw and passed right through, while the other got stuck in his head, but miraculously did not damage the eye, and stopped short a few millimeters from the brain.

Most surprising for me was the fact that the man was smiling while waiting to be taken to the operating room! I could not believe my eyes. But he was definitely smiling with a bullet in his head and a shattered jaw. Maybe he was happy that he'd been a hair away from death and had still made it; the large morphine dose he had just received probably strengthened this feeling of happiness for him.

"WATCH YOUR BACK, COUNSELOR"

Brian, a forty-year-old Black male, had a strong build and likely spent a lot of time at the gym. He had appeared in our clinic only recently and we didn't know what to make of him.

During a group session, Brian would constantly interrupt people and wouldn't let anyone squeeze a word in edgewise. It happened that I facilitated the group, and I asked him to follow the group rules. Brian ignored my directions. He was obviously high on crack.

He and I began to argue. He started openly threatening me, saying that he had recently gotten out of prison, where he had spent fifteen years behind bars for two counts of manslaughter, and that he has a black belt in Kung Fu. Of course, he called me a "white racist."

His insults got under my skin. I asked him to leave the room or else I would call the police. Brian went into a rage. He started again to talk about his black belt in Kung Fu and his two murders. He warned me that I should be careful. God forbid if I ran into him anywhere.

Until then, a patient might say that I "don't know a damn thing about real life," or I'm "book smart." But a patient had never directly threatened me before. (It is very, very rare when a patient in a drug clinic threatens a counselor or brings him any physical harm.)

I stood up, left the session room, went straight into the first open office, and called 911. At this time Brian was running around the clinic looking for me. None of the clinicians had any clue about what was going on.

After about fifteen minutes, armed cops stormed into the clinic with handcuffs and guns drawn. They dragged Brian into the hall, put him up against the wall, and searched him. Then they warned him of the consequences if something should happen to me. They told him that he could not enter the building without permission from the clinic administrator and should stay at least ten feet away from me. Then they took him outside. They gave me a special badge with a code number to use in the event of a threat or act of aggression.

Late in the evening, in my apartment, I was on the couch with my hands behind my head. I did not tell Vicky about the morning incident. She was not excited about the place I worked, and when I would get my degree she wanted me to leave the substance abuse field altogether.

I thought about what had happened that day. God knows what in Brian's words was true and what was just bullshit "high talk." I had no doubt that he had been in prison, but the two murders? Murderers, I already knew, try to keep this information private. Regardless, it was still the right thing to call the police.

All of a sudden, not related to the day's event, I remembered my childhood in Russia and how my father and I went night-fishing for catfish. My dad brought fishing poles and a tent. We made a campfire on the shore before it got too dark. I used some twigs to put a potato on the hot coals, and I watched the fire for a long time. My dad prepared the tackle so we could make the catch—the catfish is a night fish. He asked me if I would be able to stay up until midnight, or would I fall asleep? I replied confidently, "Of course, I'll stay up!" But as soon as I lay down "for a minute" inside the soft, warm sleeping bag in the tent, I closed my eyes for a moment and fell asleep. When I got out of the tent, it was sunrise and the birds were singing. My dad was standing in the water in his high rubber boots holding the pole. The fishing net held all the catfish he had caught.

Then I recalled time when my dad used to drink a lot. He worked as a mechanic at a military factory, where the majority of employees drank. Many of his coworkers also happened to live in our building.

Dad often came home drunk, sometimes accompanied by his colleagues from the factory or by neighbors. They would sit in the kitchen, drinking and chatting. I was a boy then. I still remember my mother and I intensely watching the clock every day. We knew for sure that if father hadn't returned from work by five o'clock, this meant he was drinking again, somewhere. He used to start arguments at home afterwards. Once, right in front of me, he raised his hand to my mother. Even today, after so many years, I see this terrible image as if it happened yesterday: my drunken dad grabbed my mother's shoulders and hurled her head forward. She almost fell. From that very moment, I was afraid of him. And hated him. I loved but still hated him.

I came to school with bruises under my eyes from time to time. I had to lie to my teachers and friends that I fell somewhere. I was ashamed; it seemed that the whole world still knew the truth. Dad used to attend "parent-teacher meetings" at school while drunk. In Russia parents who drank were so common that even the school didn't care much.

Fortunately, my father did not continue to drink in his later years. I don't know how and why. He did not visit any doctors or attend Alcoholics Anonymous groups. He just began to drink much less and never again got so drunk.

Did I ever forgive him for his drinking, for my crippled childhood and adolescence? Today I try to explain away his behavior, try to find answers. Occasionally I call Russia and speak to him on the phone. I often think that only now, when he has gotten old, have we become really close. But somewhere deep in my soul, like a splinter, I still have resentment and pent up anger, and there is nothing I can do about it. ...

I ran into Brian by chance the next day after he threatened me in the session and police had to escort him from the clinic with a warning to not approach me under any circumstances. I was returning home from work and walking toward my parked car. When I saw him in front of me, I stopped.

He looked emaciated and depleted. Who knows what unmentionable crap he had gotten into over the last twenty-four hours while on a crack binge? It was cold and foggy. Brian was also surprised to see me and stopped, too.

No one was around. We stood across from each other. I remembered the special police badge in my wallet. How could it help me now?

"You're the worst asshole!" Brian was looking at me, either mad or sad. "You're done, man. You're done."

He kept staring at me, and with a predatory grin, he slowly put his hand in his jacket pocket, as if reaching for a gun.

My guts froze. I was ready for the bullet to hit me. I questioned myself: "Is this the end? No, no, I don't want to die..."

At the same time, I had this reassuring feeling that nothing bad would happen, that this "grand gangster" was just making a stupid joke.

"You're lucky, asshole. I am being kind today." Brian smirked, satisfied that he had scared me. Then he cursed at me and left.

I never met him again.

OVERDOSE—ONE HUNDRED PER DAY

On average, one hundred people die per day from an opiate overdose in America. ONE HUNDRED PER DAY.

I am typing these lines now and thinking that probably, at this very moment in the United States, another person has just left this world because of drugs. Yet another hundred will be gone today. And another hundred tomorrow. And the day after tomorrow.

Death doesn't know exhaustion. Every day, with its bony hands, death from opioids overdose collects one hundred corpses of drug addicts throughout America. Both from noisy cities and from quiet suburbs. It's not only the downtrodden, never-having-worked "junkies," but also "white and blue collars" who flounder in addiction nets: lawyers, drivers, hotel administrators, construction workers, teachers. Students of colleges and even high schools.

ONE HUNDRED PER DAY.

We substance abuse counselors see this current opioids epidemic not in numbers, but in people. Sofia, Roy, Viviana, Stan, Rinaldo, Michael, James, Mark, Barbara . . . Rest in peace.

Much has been written about the current drug epidemic, and I have no intention to repeat the well-known facts here. In a few words, there is an array of causes driving the current opioid crisis. Most of the "credit" for the current opioid crisis goes to the pharmaceutical giants. These pharmaceutical monsters overfill the medical market with opiates; and from there, the pills find their way into the hands of drug dealers. High potency pills, such as fentanyl, are not just made in pharmacological factories nowadays but also in thousands of illegal laboratories across the country. Tons of fentanyl powder illegally come from China to Mexican drugs cartels, and from there are smuggled to the U.S. through the Mexican border. As a result, America is currently oversaturated with opiates.

I am finishing this book at a time when the Covid-19 epidemic is the main focus of our society which is understandable. However, this crisis has overshadowed the opioid crisis which is growing faster than ever before in the US.

Literally every day EMS cars bring people to the ED of our hospital due to opiod overdoses, they've picked them up from different places in the city; on the subway, on the stairs of a building, on a park bench, in the McDonald's restroom. Some of these people are literally at death's door; they are like corpses—gray in color, completely immobile, with open unflinching eyes.

Looking at them, I involuntarily think of Frank, who I unsuccessfully tried to save from an overdose on the beach a year ago. Now, remembering that episode, I momentarily feel a sense of powerlessness and disparity.

But under no circumstances should one in the ED indulge in sentimentality and deep philosophical thoughts. Especially now, in ED, when the time is ticking in seconds, not in minutes! Together with doctors and nurses, we transfer the patient to the stretcher and quickly take this stretcher into the Resuscitation Room. There Narcan is sprayed into his nostrils, injections are given, and a mask with an oxygen bag is put on his face. And then...

"Alive! Alive! Welcome back, buddy!"

All of us in the Resuscitation Room triumphantly high-five each other when a minute ago, the motionless body on the stretcher began to frantically shudder, the deathly pallor slowly dissipated from his face and the person began to blink.

"Yea! Here you go, buddy! Are you aware that you almost died just now by OD? Yes, fucking died. Do you understand?"

And the person on the stretcher looks around perplexed and does not understand what is going on. Where is he? Who are these people around him who are congratulating him on his "return from the other side"?

We, in the ED, are bringing back from the dead those who have been brought to us in time. What about the others, the ones to whom the EMS cars arrived too late?

ONE HUNDRED PER DAY.

EPILOGUE

I had finished university, gotten a master's degree and a social worker license, and changed jobs. I had worked in the ED at a hospital in Manhattan for a few years. My new job was located not far from the Church of St. Paul of the Apostle and Fordham University.

When I was overpowered with emotional fatigue, indifference, or anger, coming home I would enter this church. I know for sure that if you've lost faith that good prevails over evil, sooner or later, in the person's heart, you'll no longer be able to work with any patients, especially with those who suffer from drug addiction. I sat in the church on the bench, looking over the murals above the altar and on the walls. Reflections played on the golden murals, the halos of Saints glowing as light poured in through the multicolored stained glass. I would listen to solemn organ and violin music and forget about my fatigue and irritation. I don't know what happened in my soul, which unconscious forces came into play for this miracle, but it always happened this way. I would enter the temple a tired, bitter man, and leave being calm, with new hopes and faith, not feeling lonely.

Coming out of the church, I often stared at the Fordham University building across the street. I looked with gratitude and longing, regretting that my studies were over and my connection with the university was cut short.

One day when walking down the church stairs, I ran into one of my professors from Fordham. Our foreheads almost collided.

He was one of my admired professors. He was an Afro-American man, aged fifty. He was sprightly and artistic, with lively eyes. At that time, he worked as a director in a homeless shelter, while pursuing a PhD and lecturing at Fordham. This was a professor sent by God; he would charge us all with his endless energy. It was important for him that we learn and understand the material and that we, the students, felt it and appreciated it. While I was his student, I saw that he liked me, that he valued my practical knowledge. If during the class a drug addiction topic arose, he often called on me to render my opinion.

"Peter! Wow!"

"Professor! Unbelievable! Do you remember me?"

"Of course, I remember you."

I smacked him on the shoulder from happiness, like a long-lost acquaintance.

We walked down the street towards the subway station. He briefly told me about himself. He was still in Fordham teaching several classes, but he had long been a PhD, and got a top position in faculty.

"Peter, how are you?"

"Everything is ok, I got married. My daughter is two. Alas, no Ph.D., not yet. But I worked in a few clinics and crisis centers. Now I am working as a supervisor in ED. Basically, I can't complain." Unexpectedly for myself, I stopped and, frowning, cast a gloomy glance at him.

"Peter, what is the problem?" he also stopped, puzzled by my behavior. His ever-smiling, friendly face suddenly turned serious.

"You understand, Professor . . . I will tell you something. I do not think that I know absolutely everything about substance abuse.[10] But my vision and understanding of substance abuse recently started to gain some completeness. I have good professional experience to share with those who are interested. I want to teach students!" I almost screamed. "Recently, I have been researching the steps I need to take for this."

"Ok, it is good timing. Do you have a certificate as a substance abuse counselor?"

"Yes, of course, I finished substance abuse school a while back," I replied. I felt that in the depth of my chest my heart started to beat faster. I was sure this encounter with him was not an accident.

"Great. Send me your resume. We currently need a new professor for our substance abuse course. You can do it, I have no doubt, and you're gonna love it." He gave me his business card and offered me his hand to shake.

I stood rooted to the spot with my mouth wide open in surprise as if I had witnessed an unprecedented miracle. I looked after him until he was lost in the crowd of passersby entering the subway.

Later I interviewed with the Faculty Assistant to the Dean. I answered how I saw this class and how I was going to organize the lectures, and generally what I could tell the students on this subject. Then there were sleepless nights, waiting. How many times I went into Church of St. Paul the Apostle, lit candles, asking all the saints to help soften the hearts of the administrators in the Dean's office.

Early one morning, I came out of the subway on Columbus Circle. I threw my backpack behind me, with all the textbooks and folders with various papers. I slowly passed by the Time Warner skyscraper, winking at the uniformed security guard smoking on the sly by the garage. I came into Starbucks and bought myself a coffee. I had an hour left until class. In an hour my first lecture would begin.

I drank coffee, reviewing the pages with my notes for the umpteenth time. "What students will I have in my class? Why did they choose this class? Will I be able to convey to them what I know and how I understand drug addiction? What do I do about my Russian accent? What about my complete lack of teaching experience? Ah!"

Finishing my coffee, I left the café and soon stood before the University entrance. Students and teachers streamed through the wide glass doors.

I stood by those doors. And my whole life in America flashed before my eyes. I recalled the time when I attended the substance abuse counselor school, how I worked in Francesca's clinic, and then in the hospital while studying at Fordham. I recalled the many patients, coworkers, and professors which I have met throughout the years.

Our whole life consists of serendipitous encounters. And these seemingly unexpected meetings influence us, form us, and open our hearts to new depths and make us who we were meant to become.

"Oh Lord, won't you buy me a Mercedes Benz? ..."

FOOTNOTES AND AUTHOR COMMENTARY

[1]This sense of unique kinship among users and alcoholics was the driving force of establishing Alcoholics Anonymous (AA) and later Narcotics Anonymous (NA). For almost a century now, this fellowship continues to save the lives of countless addicts worldwide. We may recall the founding of this movement in a nutshell: the famous Bill Wilson, an unsuccessful Wall Street broker and chronic alcoholic, wound up in mental hospitals with delirium tremens on more than one occasion. All the doctors refused to treat him, believing Bill to be a hopeless case. One day, at the house of a priest, he met another "hopeless" alcoholic like him (Doctor Bob). They shared their secret lives of alcoholism with each other. They separated that evening, convinced that alcoholics could not only pour drinks for each other or bury each other, but also could save one another. Thus, a movement was born.

[2]An "active" drug user is one who currently uses drugs.

[3]Notions such as "Don't go to extremes," "think about negative consequences," "don't speculate about the distant future, don't dwell on past, and live one day at a time," and so on come from the same source of wisdom. There is a universal set of rules, a kind of "Addict's Book of Wisdom" for those who wish to recover. These rules and approaches to life are repeated in

each substance abuse clinic and 12-step meeting. Drug users hear these principles and slogans dozens, hundreds, thousands of times, with the intention to practice them in daily life.

[4] The measures taken to treat patients in those first rehab clinics were, by today's standards, draconian and resembled those used in prisons. Patients there were forced to carry out difficult and, at times, completely pointless jobs. They would be kicked out or punished for even the tiniest infractions. However, in addition to strict daily routines and labor, the techniques of group psychotherapy were also introduced. The goal was not to demean or punish, but to teach humility, to teach the drug user to listen and hear others, to admit defeat and bankruptcy of his erroneous twisted philosophy.

[5] All joking aside, the average salary of an ordinary substance abuse counselor or social worker in the substance abuse field is about 35-55K a year—not a lot when considering the enormous psychological burden he/she has to withstand.

[6] In the substance abuse field, the word "codependency" is often mentioned. This is a condition whereby a person ceases to take an interest in his own life and fully immerses himself in the sickness of another person. Codependency is often even more resistant and harder to treat than addiction itself. Self-help Al-Anon groups exist for people with codependency, who are "sick from the disease" of their children, spouse, or any significant other. People do not attend to learn how to treat their addicted child or wife. The goal is different: to learn how not to live through another's disease, but to live one's own life.

[7] Some people believe that the only sure way is to kick the addict out of the house, and so then everything will be solved. This remedy does not always have a curative effect. Sometimes this way works, but sometimes it doesn't. First, not every parent or spouse is capable of taking such a drastic step. Obviously, this is a family member, not a withering plant. How do you throw someone you love out on the street? Second, a drug user who finds himself on the street will not necessarily stop using. In fact, the opposite will likely happen: The person begins to use more,

loses his skills for living in society, and quickly enters the world of criminality. Or he may be killed by his fellow users for a bag of dope or a crack rock.

[8]The subject "drug addiction-mental health" is very complicated and requires some level of reader preparedness. Therefore, I decided not to touch this topic in this book.

[9]It is important to remember that almost every drug user basically wants to stop using. It's very uncommon to meet a drug user who doesn't want to stop. But at the same time, he also sincerely wants to continue getting high. Besides the physical craving and fear of withdrawal, another fear pulls at him. Fear of change. Fear of failure. Fear of crawling out of his dark little world of misery. In this dangerous little world, everything is painful, but it is familiar. It is also possible to get used to the pain. It's no coincidence that drug users call this world of misery a "comfort zone." There comes a time, however, when the emotional and physical pain reaches its limit, and being in the "comfort zone" becomes unbearable. At this time, he becomes willing and ready to make changes in order to move out from this "zone."

[10] What is drug addiction? Why does a person become a drug addict or alcoholic? Those who are interested can open the last edition of Diagnostic and Statistical Manual of Mental Disorders, where the symptoms and diagnosis of alcohol/drug addiction are outlined in detail. Shortly, this is what evidence-based practice has to say about alcohol/drug addiction—it's a chronic, progressive disease that is characterized by relapses. Once addicted, a person is left with this addiction for life, regardless of how long they remain sober. This means that after even ten or twenty years of sobriety, a person retains that dependency. The first shot they drink or the first bag of drugs they shoot will very likely return them quickly to the same pit which was so difficult to climb out of long ago.

What are the main symptoms of alcohol/drug addiction? First of all, the consumption of either **causes serious problems** with a person's family, work, and health—basically, in all areas of their life—but despite this, they will still continue to use/drink. Regardless of their many desperate attempts, they are **not able to control** or manage their drinking/drugging.

Then, it causes **withdrawal syndrome**. Thus, within some time after using drugs/alcohol, when the high wears off, the person almost always feels physiological or psychological (or both) withdrawals and experiences headaches, heavy sweats, nervousness, depressed state, etc.

Then, their **tolerance** level increases. In other words, in order to experience the same high, the drug/alcohol dosage has to constantly increase.

A prolonged intense usage of narcotic substances causes irreversible damage to brain function and leads to complications with the endocrine, cardiovascular, and all other systems of the human body.

Why does a person become a drug addict/alcoholic? It is a well-known and proven theory that there is a hereditary and genetic affinity for alcohol/drugs. It is also known that alcohol/drugs help a person to deal with various difficult mental conditions such as depression, anxiety, mood swings, etc. Those who have these problems sometimes start to use drugs as a remedy or self-medication. This process of healing one illness may lead to the emergence of another. Developing alcohol/drug addiction could also be based on the physiological makeup of a particular individual, depending on how their liver metabolizes alcohol and drugs, along with malnutrition and vitamin deficiency. It can also be a neurobiological reason, depending on how a person's brain reacts to psychoactive substances.

Many people become dependent on drugs/alcohol for psychosocial reasons. It can be said with certainty that experience of emotional traumas, sexual abuse, rape, and prolonged stress connected to socio-economic environments (life in areas with high criminality, family poverty, the sudden death of a loved one, racism, xenophobia, homophobia, offenses and torture on any grounds) negatively impact the development and contribute to addiction.

Very often developing drug/alcohol addiction is caused by a combination of the several reasons. Sometimes the main reason still remains unclear.

Treatment of addiction may consist of different ways, including psychotherapy, medication, dieting, religious and spiritual, traditional and not traditional healings, etc.—all depending on the situation, availability of the treatment options and remedies, and individual response.

ABOUT THE AUTHOR

Petr Nemirovskiy was born in 1963 in Kiev, Ukraine. He graduated from Kiev University with a degree in journalism, and began his career as a journalist and writer.

He has lived in the United States since 1995. He graduated from Fordham University in the U.S. with a Master's of Clinical Social Work and has been working as a psychotherapist specializing in the field of drug addiction for more than fifteen years.

He also works as professor of Social Work Practice with Substance Use Disorders at Fordham University.

With his new novel, *A Walk Down Misery Street*, Petr Nemirovskiy shows his talents as both a writer and a professional substance abuse clinician.

www.ingramcontent.com/pod-product-compliance
Lightning Source LLC
Chambersburg PA
CBHW071238070526
44583CB00017B/2238